A CENTURY OF

PUNCH

A CENTURY OF

WILLIAM HEINEMANN LTD

MELBOURNE LONDON TORONTO

Published in 1956

by William Heinemann Ltd

99 Great Russell Street, London, WC1

Printed in Great Britain by

Jarrold & Sons Limited, Norwich

For all people of good humour

Contents

Preface

❊

THANK YOU FOR STARTING HERE. I usually skip prefaces and I have a feeling that most other people do too, but this one may help your enjoyment of this book, so be patient for a few pages, please.

Every book on, or of, humour inevitably starts with its editor or author attempting to define humour or declining to do so and getting around to it in the finish just the same.

My definition is here, committed in the next 344 pages, and if yours is approximately the same you will enjoy the cartoons in this book, and if not, then snip off the price on the jacket and send this book on its way as a gift to someone deserving of it.

PUNCH has come out every week for the last 115 years and during that time has published something like 90,000 joke drawings. During its earliest days PUNCH was more famous for its politics than its humour, and its political cartoons, sometimes statesmanlike, often malicious, wielded a power that any newspaper chain would envy today even though PUNCH's circulation was only a few thousands. In between the castigation of Prime Ministers, foreign powers, the Prince Consort, and the then un-United States of America, PUNCH fulfilled the promise made in the introduction to the first volume in 1841 that it would be a refuge for "destitute wit", for "orphan jokes" and "perishing puns". The destitute wit soon got off the bread line when the first PUNCH artists—of exceptional calibre—took it in hand, and the orphan jokes made up for their lack of ancestry by begetting a line of descendants that bear the family likeness to this day. The puns luckily did perish.

After a few years there emerged the style of joke for which PUNCH became famous (or notorious), and H. F. Ellis, a Literary Editor of PUNCH, sums it up neatly in a piece disparaging the literacy of comic artists:

> During the second half of the nineteenth century, and even later, writers wrote the jokes and artists drew the pictures that roughly corresponded with the situation envisaged. That the legends must have been the work of writers is proved by their length and complexity: from six to eight lines of dialogue, involving up to four characters and the use of such advanced symbols as semicolons, brackets and italicised exclamation marks—this is clearly beyond the compass of any but an educated man. Nor was the division of labour altogether unfair. The artist faced the problem of portraying in a single drawing the interchange of conversation lasting several minutes and ranging over the whole gamut of human emotions. Not for him the simple modern trick of indicating the speaker by an open mouth or a touch of black. Where all spoke, and some more than once, his only recourse was to keep all mouths shut and make all his characters

AUTHOR'S MISERIES

Old Gentleman. Miss Wiggets. Two Authors

Old Gentleman: "I AM SORRY TO SEE YOU OCCUPIED, MY DEAR MISS WIGGETS, WITH THAT TRIVIAL PAPER 'PUNCH.' A RAILWAY IS NOT A PLACE, IN MY OPINION, FOR JOKES. I NEVER JOKE—NEVER."

Miss W: "SO I SHOULD THINK, SIR."

Old Gentleman: "AND BESIDES, ARE YOU AWARE WHO ARE THE CONDUCTORS OF THAT PAPER, AND THAT THEY ARE CHARTISTS, DEISTS, ATHEISTS, ANARCHISTS, AND SOCIALISTS, TO A MAN? I HAVE IT FROM THE BEST AUTHORITY, THAT THEY MEET TOGETHER ONCE A WEEK IN A TAVERN IN SAINT GILE'S, WHERE THEY CONCOCT THEIR INFAMOUS PRINT. THE CHIEF PART OF THEIR INCOME IS DERIVED FROM THREATENING LETTERS WHICH THEY SEND TO THE NOBILITY AND GENTRY. THE PRINCIPAL WRITER IS A RETURNED CONVICT. TWO HAVE BEEN TRIED AT THE OLD BAILEY; AND THEIR ARTIST—AS FOR THEIR ARTIST. . . .

Guard: SWIN-DUN! STA-TION!"

(*Exeunt two Authors*)

(1848)

---

black, or blackish. This helped the reader to concentrate all his attention—and be sure he needed it—on the joke itself.

He continues rather acidly:

This happy collaboration of writer and artist ended when artists, in obedience to the new creed of self-sufficiency, decided to launch out on their own. "We will write," they declared, "our own legends." At once—and America has been blamed for this, in my view unfairly—the legend dropped to a single line, and even this is proving too much for contemporary artists. The written word is disappearing from comic art. More. The drawing itself is tending to follow it, and has in many cases, as the reader, or rather looker, may discover for himself, all but gone. Perfection cannot now be far off.

(1946)

This book contains the drawing with the eight-line caption and that which tells its story speechlessly. Let the reader here be warned—or reassured—this book has none of the political side of PUNCH in it. It does not purport to be a social history. The compilation is for fun, and if you are not amused it will have failed in its purpose.

There have been anthologies, histories, even libraries of humour taken from the contents of PUNCH, but never before has there been contained in one volume a sampling of the cartoon humour stretching over the whole period of PUNCH's existence.

The sole principle used in the choice was that the cartoon should still appear funny today. This has meant ignoring all local and topical references and choosing very thinly from certain subjects that had them rolling in the aisles in the Victorian era.

Let's face it that, despite its early radicalism, PUNCH found much of its humour in snobbishness and class consciousness, and it is a humour that does not carry well over a century. Servant girls were flayed for their stupidity, ignorance and presumption, and flunkeys, more understandably, for their idleness and their aping of their masters. A casual student of the old PUNCH pictures might justifiably have thought that Britain was one large hunting field, judging by the number of jokes on the subject that appeared. The artist and "gag merchant" of today need not be embarrassed by their addiction to variations in the current cartoon clichés such as the desert island, the hole in the ice, the psychiatrist's couch and lately the arriving Martians. They can never be as single-minded as Mr. Punch was on the question of hunting. There was the gentleman who had been unseated and there was the gentleman who had no intention of taking the gate or fence in front of him. On those themes hang many, many cartoons that you will not find in this book. Many of them were exquisitely drawn and it was a struggle not to include them for that reason.

Luckily it has been possible to do full justice to those wonderful artists of the Victorian era who drew directly on the wood in pen or pencil for the engraver to do his skilled but uninspired best with, because they also dealt in the immutable gold of the humour of human nature that is acceptable today from Chaucer, Shakespeare, Victorian PUNCH or possibly from the strips of your daily newspaper.

It is possible that you have been drawn to this book with the hope of belly laughs and perhaps you have a slightly uneasy feeling, increased by this preface, that you will have to work for them. Therefore it is in order to explain what has been done for your comfort in this book.

It has been put into sections and each section is a main subject for joking, and practically all the subjects are of interest to people who love, marry, have children and cars, call in the doctor and go to the cinema and the theatre. These subjects, and others, have their own chronology in this book. On each subject you may see the fashion in humour, the fashion in drawing changing through the years.

"He says he's lost." (1953)

The painstaking drawing and the leisurely caption were indicative of the time when they were used. There was more time to read and there were fewer magazines. There was time to let a joke soak in. The characters in the pictures were real and reached their height in reality, humour and draftsmanship in the efforts of Phil May, who anticipated by thirty years the economy of line in comic drawing that has now been carried to such an extreme that the human figure is sometimes little more than a symbol and the drawing gets by with the wit of its caption or fun of its situation.

The modern magazine riffler expects and accepts this shorthand humour. It is in tune with his mood and the time he has to spare. He must vary his pace in going through this book and soak in some of the jokes as the Victorians did. He will find it worth while. I did.

The biggest section in the book is that which deals with war and its effect on the civilian and the uniformed. The British are at their best in extracting humour from crises and unfunny happenings. There was an abundance of these between 1914 and 1918 and again between 1939 and 1945. At such times PUNCH is also at its best and has the common touch that is not always so apparent when the national life is safe and humdrum.

It may be as well to sketch in lightly the background from which these thousand cartoons have been plucked. (Anyone not background-minded should now pass on to the cartoons.)

In the City of London, in the precinct of the Abbey of Whitefriars, in Bouverie Street, just off Fleet Street is PUNCH office, a modest red-brick building of five stories. The street is narrow, usually blocked with trucks unloading paper for the 8,000,000-circulation *News of the World* opposite and noisy with scuttling vans of the evening *Star* (circulation 1,000,000). Once through the door of PUNCH (circulation 150,000), there is a country-house peace, and it is a surprise that no butler greets you but instead a commissionaire who himself looks a little like Mr. Punch. He will unhurriedly get your name wrong and, should you have legitimate business, lead you up the graceful sweep of dangerously polished stairs. You may catch a glimpse of the present Editor-in-chief Malcolm Muggeridge, who after three years in the chair also looks like Mr. Punch.

Phil May

Dooley: "WHAT'S THE MATTER WID YE ANYHOW, MICK—ALL TATTERED AN' TORRUN AN' BITTEN AN' SCRATCHED ALL OVER?"
Mick: "AY, AN' ME OWN DOG DONE IT! I WANT HOME SOBER LAST NOIGHT, AN' THE BASTE DIDN'T KNOW ME!"

(1901)

On the Editorial floor you will find, with luck, seven editors and three secretaries at work. There is complaint of overcrowding, for until 1946 the main editorial business was carried out by an editor-in-chief, an art editor and two assistant editors who vied for the services of one secretary.

PUNCH has been on this site since Bradbury and Evans, Printers, bought it and its debts for £300 in 1843, two years after PUNCH's struggling start. Bradbury and Evans were also successful publishers. They published both Charles Dickens and Thackeray's works, *The Field*, and also the *Daily News*. Their buying of PUNCH was more due to the persuasiveness of its cashless owners than wise anticipation of its future, unique in fortune and fame. Today, Bradbury and Agnew (Evans dropped out in the 70s) spend all their time in publishing PUNCH and the quarterly *The Countryman*.

Twenty-five pounds was the capital for launching PUNCH. Ebenezer Landells, an engraver, was the man with the original idea. He wanted a paper that was the equivalent of the Paris *Charivari*, a satirical journal that gave plenty of scope to a skilled engraver. Without any mechanical processes in those days the engraver was of importance equal to, if not greater than, the artist, The first editor was Mark Lemon, a tavern-keeper, who had failed to make his tavern pay. His heart was in writing, chiefly for the stage, and he was existing on £100 for a comedy accepted for the London stage when PUNCH gave him permanent employment. His love of the theatre persisted through all twenty-nine years of his editorship, and the PUNCH amateur theatricals written, produced and acted in by the PUNCH staff and contributors (some of them unwillingly) often occupied more time than the production of PUNCH.

PUNCH sold 6,000 copies a week until it published the first annual Almanack number. This sold 90,000 copies, and the romantic fact of its success was that it was mostly written in the Fleet debtors prison where Harry Grattan, a prominent contributor, was incarcerated, and where Henry Mayhew, a PUNCH founder, contrived to spend a week with him without benefit of sentence. One other event set PUNCH on its way to success, and this, incongruously enough for a comic paper, was a long tragic poem entitled "The Song of the Shirt" by Thomas Hood. It lamented the plight of women shirtmakers who were paid the sum of five farthings for sewing a shirt. The poem trebled the sale of PUNCH.

From then on PUNCH's success was due to its trenchant cartoons and articles representing a large body of public opinion on social and political problems, and usually representing the whole of the nation's feelings on international events. I think it is true to say that as PUNCH's political power waned, so more attention was paid to the humorous side.

When mechanical methods of engraving were introduced there was greater ease in production of cartoons. This coincided with the emergence of a group of artists more suited to getting fun out of the social scene than the political one. And the era ended when PUNCH was regularly banned from France and Germany, when British governments trembled at what PUNCH might say, and Prime Ministers tried to curry favour with PUNCH cartoonists with the hope of a more flattering presentation of themselves.

PUNCH settled in to be dull and respectable, with flashes of brilliance. Its pages were usually more entertaining to look at in retrospect rather than week by week.

PUNCH of the early 1900s was scholarly but uninspired, but with the 1914-18 war it came into its trenchant own again as a morale-raiser. It so exacerbated the Kaiser that he put a price on the editor's head. Between the wars it was prim and gentle, but its team of artists—which included Fougasse, Bateman, George Belcher, Frank Reynolds and Pont—was so strong in humour that its weakness in other directions was hardly noticed. It was during this period that it became one of the most successful advertising media in the country.

"I said, if you don't mind we'll just put you down as a 'Don't know.'"

(1947)

Came World War II, and Fougasse and David Langdon were chief among those taking the sting out of the grimmest happenings. Emett supplied the fantasy, and some sixty artists kept up regular submissions no matter to which wartime occupation they were called.

Today PUNCH has returned to political satire and extreme topicality, and whoever edits the second *Century of* PUNCH in 2055 will have no trouble over hunting jokes or unrest among the domestics.

If you are still with me stay a little longer, for I do not think I should finish without saying a word or two about the three giants who support the early pages in each section of the book. They are John Leech, Charles Keene and George du Maurier. Each of them contributed something over 3,000 drawings to PUNCH. Leech was there from the start, and apart from a few months when he had a one-man strike for higher pay his drawings appeared regularly for twenty-three years. In one Almanack he was responsible for twenty-two of the twenty-four drawings in it. Halfway through his medical studies his father failed in business and Leech the younger had to earn his own living. After assisting a doctor for a year or two he turned to art and was not long in establishing himself. His was a generous disposition and twice he found himself for a short period in prison through the failure of friends to meet bills that he had backed for them. At twenty-two he saw his future wife for the first time in the street, followed her home, found her name in the directory, arranged an introduction and swiftly married her. She appears over and over again in his drawings. Leech and PUNCH went up in the social scale together. "Mr. Leech," said Thackeray, "surveys society from the gentleman's point of view." This did not prevent his steady work in the paper against poverty and oppression. His most famous cartoon character was Mr. Briggs, who was a middle-

John Leech

Juvenile: "DO YOU OBJECT TO MY SMOKING A CIGAR, SIR?"
Elderly Party: "OH NO, CERTAINLY NOT, IF IT DOESN'T MAKE YOU SICK!"

(1859)

class British householder, a bit simple-minded, with plenty of pluck and something of a sportsman. He was based on Leech's own experiences.

Leech was fond of hunting, abnormally frightened of noise, a model of propriety. He died at forty-seven, and though he had been earning £2,000 a year for some years—very high pay in those days—he died penniless and neither his family nor his friends knew where his money had gone. A Civil List pension was granted to his widow chiefly through the efforts of Disraeli, who had often been pilloried unmercifully by Leech in his cartoons.

Charles Keene was always credited with having some of the best drawings and worst jokes in Punch. As Phil May said later, "He was the Daddy of us all" as regards drawing, and even the best of engravers could not do justice to his art with the crude wood block. He joined Punch ten years after Leech and could have made his name as a water-colourist or in oils had he so chosen, but his principal work was for Punch, and in contrast to Leech he died leaving £30,000. He was a bachelor and lived a Bohemian life with an untidy studio where he ate sweets and sausages together. Haggis, black pudding, and bouillabaisse were his favourite dishes. He played the guitar, the recorder and the bagpipes. Among his interests were birds and animals, flint arrowheads, sailing and soldiers—so writes his biographer. He died at sixty-eight.

George Louis Palmella Busson du Maurier joined Punch nine years after Keene and owed a lot to his friendship with him. Whether British womanhood changed from the rather dumpy representations of Leech

Du Maurier

He: "THAT'S MRS. GRIMSHAW, WHO LECTURES ON BIMETALLISM. I'VE HEARD HER. HOW EXASPERATINGLY CLEVER SHE SEEMS TO BE!"
She: "YES—BUT HOW CONSOLINGLY UGLY!"

(1895)

to the tall, gracious women of Du Maurier in such a few years is open to doubt, but Du Maurier was the apostle of grace in PUNCH's pages, leaving the more boisterous fun to other people. His noble creatures, male and female, had a certain lack of variety, but his pictures of the way of life of the English upper class are accepted as standard for the late Victorian era. But one is apt to overlook the incisiveness of his satires on the precious and affected types of his day. Besides the captions to his drawings he wrote novels, and his famous *Trilby* is read to this day.

His name has been carried on in famous manner, for Sir Gerald du Maurier, the actor, was his son, and Daphne du Maurier, his granddaughter, has followed his tradition in writing best-selling novels.

Among the host of modern artists I must mention four, who not only stand out as superb artists in their own genre, but as Art Editors of PUNCH have so greatly influenced the style and content of PUNCH drawings. They are F. H. Townsend (Art Editor 1905-20), Frank Reynolds (Art Editor 1920-31), both now dead, Kenneth Bird (Fougasse) (Art Editor 1937-49) and Russell Brockbank, the present Art Editor.

An innate gentleness of nature common to all of them has made them eminently suited to dealing with that sensitive creature the humorous artist. When I think of the 50,000 drawings that these four gentlemen have accepted for PUNCH my mind boggles at the number of "Sorry—not quite's" they have had to hand out by letter, telephone and in person. They have all lessened the harshness of the rejection slip whenever they could. Thank you, gentlemen, for the *embarras de richesse* from which I have made my later choice.

The temptation is to go on with a word or two about the other 200 artists whose work you will find in this book. But you must have had enough. So press on!

R. E. WILLIAMS

ACKNOWLEDGMENTS

To Bradbury, Agnew & Company, Ltd., the Proprietors of PUNCH, for close co-operation on all matters pertaining to this book.

To Smilby for his original decorations for the individual sections.

To H. Noel Wood for generous technical assistance in the layout.

PEOPLE AT WORK . . .

OR NEARLY!

People who work sitting down get paid more than people who work standing up.

OGDEN NASH 1938

I like work; it fascinates me. I can sit and look at it for hours.

JEROME K. JEROME 1889

"The trouble is, me and 'im don't see eye to eye."
(1948)

Navvy: "WHY DON'T YER WEAR THEM BOARDS THE RIGHT WAY ROUND?"
Sandwichman: "WOT! IN ME DINNER-HOUR? NOT ME!"

(1920)

Working Man sitting on the steps of a big house in, say, Russell Square, smoking pipe. A mate passes by with plumbing tools, etc.
Man with tools: "HULLO, JIM! WOT ARE YER DOIN' 'ERE? CARETAKIN'?"
Man on steps: "NO. I'M THE HOWNER, 'ERE."
Man with tools: "'OW'S THAT?"
Man on steps: "WHY, I DID A BIT O' PLUMBING IN THE 'OUSE, AN' I TOOK THE PLACE IN PART PAYMENT FOR THE JOB."

(1901)

Sympathetic Passer-by: "BUT IF HE'S BADLY HURT, WHY DOESN'T HE GO TO THE HOSPITAL?"
British Workman: "WOT! IN 'IS DINNER-TIME!!"

(1896)

"LOR, BILL, WE'VE GOT INTO A FUST-CLAWSS CARRIAGE."
"YER DON'T SAY SO! AND ME WIV ODD SOCKS ON!"

(1909)

Lady: "I DO HOPE YOU'LL GET THE BATH DONE SOON. IT'S REALLY MOST INCONVENIENT."
Plumber: "WE'LL DO OUR BEST, LADY. WHEN'S YER BATH-NIGHT?"

(1932)

THE LABOUR QUESTION

Mechanic: "HULLO, JEM, NOT AT WORK! WHAT'S UP?"

Collier: "OH, WE'RE OUT ON STRIKE."

Mechanic: "WHAT FOR, THEN?"

Collier: "AW DIVEN' KNAW, BUT WE'LL NOT GIVE IN TILL WE GET IT!"

(1889)

"WHERE'S YER FATHER? 'AS 'E GONE TO WORK?"

"I SEE 'IM GOIN' DAHN THE STREET, BUT 'E WASN'T GOIN' TO WORK."

" 'OW D'YOU KNOW?"

"WELL, 'E WERE RUNNIN'."

(1925)

The Plumber: " 'E SAYS TER ME 'I WANTS THE SINK IN THE CORNER,' 'E SAYS, AND I SAYS, ' 'OO D'YER FINK YOU ARE?' AND 'E SAYS, 'WELL, I'M THE BLOKE WOT'S PAYIN' FER THE JOB,' 'E SAYS, AND I SAYS, 'THEN KEEP YER PLACE,' I SAYS."

(1930)

Lazy Husband: "I SEE THERE'S TALK OF ANOTHER STRIKE."

Wife: "YES; AN' IF YOU WAS 'ARF A MAN YOU'D GET A JOB AN' BE ABLE TO GO ON STRIKE TOO."

(1925)

Plumber (with dignity, as the lady of the house interrupts his work): "AFORE YOU SPEAKS, MUM, I'LL TELL YOU I KNOWS ALL THE JOKES CONCERNIN' MY PERFESSION. I'VE GOT ALL ME TOOLS 'ERE—I REMAINS TILL I'VE LOCATED THE LEAKAGE—I AIN'T GOIN' BACK FER NOTHIN' AND I AIN'T GOT NO MATE."

Lady: "BUT THERE'S NOTHING THE MATTER HERE. YOU'VE COME TO THE WRONG HOUSE."

(1931)

Indignant Householder: "YOU'VE PAPERED THE STUDY WITH THE BATHROOM PAPER AND THE BATHROOM WITH THE STUDY PAPER. WHAT DO YOU PROPOSE TO DO ABOUT IT?"

Paperhanger: "DUNNO, SIR. I'D WILLINGLY SHIFT THE BATH FOR YOU, BUT THAT'S A PLUMBER'S JOB."

(1929)

"NOW THERE'S NO NEED TO FOLLOW ME UP 'ERE, MA'AM. I CAN GET ON MUCH BETTER IF I AIN'T WATCHED."

(1932)

"I've tested this new drill, sir. It seems to be all right."

(1934)

Country Cousin (after prolonged inspection of building operations): "I DON'T SEE THE SENSE OF PUTTING STATUES ON THE TOP OF YOUR BUILDINGS."

Friend: "STATUES? THOSE AREN'T STATUES—THEY'RE BRICKLAYERS."

(1925)

Foreman Builder: "NOW THEN, YOU; HURRY UP, CAN'T YER!"

Labourer: "ORL RIGHT, BOSS; ROME WASN'T BUILT IN A DAY."

Foreman Builder: "NO, P'R'APS NOT; BUT I WASN'T FOREMAN O' THAT JOB."

(1913)

"Well, here's the last of the January jobs, Fred—No. 91 Church Street—burst pipe."

(1941)

POPULAR MISCONCEPTIONS
BRITISH BUSINESS METHODS

(1938)

Employer: "LOOK AT THIS LETTER FROM MESSRS. SMITH, BEAUTIFULLY TYPED."
Typist: "UM—AND THE GRAMMAR'S EXCELLENT TOO."

(1932)

Clerk to Office Boy (after Senior Partner has told poor joke): "WHY DON'T YOU LAUGH TOO?"
Office Boy: "I DON'T NEED TO; I'M LEAVING ON SATURDAY."

(1911)

"*Miss Cartright in here is having to do the work of two people.*"
(1951)

"*Every now and then it makes a noise exactly like a shoulder-strap breaking.*"
(1948)

"*I was the Chairman of the Board until I found out about the rates for overtime.*"
(1946)

"*Let's see now, last year I was away in June.*"
(1954)

"*Sometimes I think it will drive me mad.*"
(1949)

"*And the whole idea of this winter holiday was to keep my mind off the Sales Chart.*"
(1936)

"Why are all the letters different?"

(1950)

"Now, if all three are there, he's somewhere around the office. If the hat's gone, he's at elevenses: if the hat and umbrella's gone he's at lunch; if they've all gone, he's left for the day."

(1949)

"Of course I still love you. It's just that it's not convenient to discuss it at the moment."

(1950)

"*I know it's very gratifying to have you model yourself on my lines, Mr. Crankshott . . .*"

(1940)

"*Well, what did the old skinflint say when you asked him for a rise?*"

(1946)

CLOTHES CONSCIOUS

When you have looked through this book you will have a good idea of what the British have been wearing over the last century. The next 23 pictures, however, have been grouped as they make amusing comment on a few of the extremes in fashion of yesteryear.

A POSER FOR A BLOOMER

Old Gentleman: "BEFORE I CAN ENTERTAIN YOUR PROPOSAL, AND GIVE MY CONSENT TO YOUR MARRYING MY SON, I MUST ASK YOU, WHETHER YOU ARE IN A POSITION—A—TO—A—KEEP HIM IN THE STYLE TO WHICH—A—I MAY SAY—HE HAS ALWAYS BEEN ACCUSTOMED? AHEM!"

(1853)

THE LAST NEW FAD. A REACTION FROM ESTHETICS.

The Professor: "NOW, LADIES. STRAIGHT FROM THE SHOULDER, PLEASE!—AND DON'T TRY TO SCRATCH—'TAIN'T NO GOOD WITH THE GLOVES ON!"

M. le Professeur: "ALLONS, MADEMOISELLE,—VIF LA! ROMPEZ—PARADE ET RIPOSTE EN QUARTE. BON! ENCORE UNE FOIS LA FEINTE DE SECONDE. HARDI! UNE, DEUSSE, TROISSE! FENDEZ-VOUS BIEN,—PARFAIT!"

(1856)

COMMON OBJECTS AT THE SEASIDE—GENERALLY FOUND UPON THE ROCKS AT LOW WATER

(1858)

MERMAIDS AT PLAY; OR, A NICE LITTLE WATER PARTY

(1847)

NEW OMNIBUS REGULATION
"*Werry sorry'm, but yer'l 'av to leave yer Krinerline outside.*"

(1858)

"*Polite Rustic:* "OH! AFTER YOU, MUM."

(1858)

(1954)

Old Gentleman (shocked beyond description) to Verger: "DON'T YOU THINK THOSE YOUTHS HAD BETTER BE TOLD TO TAKE THEIR HATS OFF?"

Verger: "TAKE THEIR 'ATS OFF! BLESS YOU, SIR, THOSE ARE THE DEAN'S YOUNG LADIES!"

1877

1862

Enter Mamma and Aunt Ellen

Mamma (to Old Woman): "PRAY, HAVE YOU MET TWO LADIES AND A GENTLEMAN?"

Old Woman: "WELL, I MET THREE PEOPLE—BUT, LA! THERE, I CAN'T TELL LADIES FROM GENTLEMEN NOW-A-DAYS—WHEN I WAS A GAL, &C., &C."

1896

The Vicar of St. Winifred-in-the-Wold (to fair Bicyclists): "IT IS CUSTOMARY FOR MEN, I WILL NOT SAY GENTLEMEN, TO REMOVE THEIR HATS ON ENTERING A CHURCH!"

Confusion of the Ladies Rota and Ixiona Bykewell.

SOME LADIES HAVE TAKEN TO WEARING JERSEYS—AND VERY HEALTHY AND BECOMING THEY ARE! NOW, WHY SHOULD NOT GENTLEMEN CONTENT THEMSELVES WITH MERE UNDERCLOTHING, AND DISCARD THE HIDEOUS CHIMNEY-POT, FROCK-COAT, AND TROUSERS OF THE PERIOD, SO FATAL TO PICTORIAL DESIGN? (N. B.—THE UNDER-VEST TO BE WORN OUTSIDE THE DRAWERS. ÇA VA SANS DIRE!) (1880)

OF AN EVENING, THE VEST, DRAWERS, AND SOCKS MIGHT BE BLACK. WHAT MORE CALCULATED TO SHOW OFF A FINE FIGURE! BESIDES WHICH, IT WOULD BE A NATIONAL COSTUME, SINCE NO COUNTRY CAN VIE WITH OURS IN THE ELEGANCE OF ITS UNDERCLOTHING. (1880)

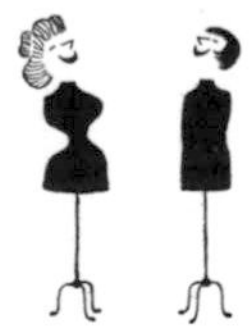

THE NEW EXPRESSION

AN ATTITUDE OBSERVABLE IN YOUNG LADIES OF TO-DAY AT CHURCH PARADE AND ELSEWHERE IS SUPPOSED TO BE THE RESULT OF CONSTANT DEVOTION TO THE BICYCLE.

(1896)

DEA EX MACHINA!

(1891)

SUBACIDITIES

Gladys: "OH, MURIEL DEAR, THAT HEAVENLY FROCK!—I THINK IT LOOKS LOVELIER EVERY YEAR!"

(1893)

A SKETCH FROM NATURE

(1884)

"HULLO, GERTY! YOU'VE GOT FRED'S HAT ON, AND HIS COVER COAT?"
"YES. DON'T YOU LIKE IT?"
"WELL—IT MAKES YOU LOOK LIKE A YOUNG MAN, YOU KNOW, AND THAT'S SO EFFEMINATE!"

(1891)

THE ELECTRIC LIGHT, SO FAVOURABLE TO FURNITURE, WALL PAPERS, PICTURES, SCREENS, &C., IS NOT ALWAYS BECOMING TO THE FEMALE COMPLEXION. LIGHT JAPANESE SUNSHADES WILL BE FOUND INVALUABLE.

(1889)

Diehard (stroking his beard): "MY DEAR GIRL, IT'S OUR ONLY CHANCE LEFT. AS SOON AS YOU CAN IMITATE THIS WE'RE DONE."

(1925)

"WILL YE TAK' THE PAPER?"
"THANKS. I DON'T CARE FOR READING IN THE TRAIN."
"MAYBE. BUT WILL YE KINDLY COVER YER KNEES WI' IT? A'VE NAE WISH TO CONTEMPLATE THEM."

(1927)

Husband: "I SHOULD HAVE THOUGHT YOU'D BE ASHAMED TO SHOW YOUR FACE IN SUCH A GOWN."
Wife: "DON'T WORRY, DARLING. MY FACE WON'T BE THE CHIEF ATTRACTION."

(1929)

Kindly Old Soul: "LOST YOUR MOTHER, HAVE YOU? WHY DIDN'T YOU HANG ON TO HER SKIRTS?"
Small Boy: "I COULDN'T REACH 'EM."

(1925)

Anton

ANIMALS . . .
DUMB
AND
NOT SO
DUMB

Animals started to talk in PUNCH in the 30s, but there were one or two forerunners —notably a very succinct bull (p. 42). The fairest jokes of this type are those which appear merely to translate the animal's thoughts to our own language.

"It's your friend Rover again."
(1947)

THE PUP—WHAT WILL HE BECOME?

WHEN I BOUGHT HIM AS A PUPPY AND THE MAN SAID—

HE WOULD GROW—

INTO A VERY—

FINE HOUSE-DOG—

I FORGOT TO TELL HIM—

I LIVE IN A VERY SMALL FLAT.

(1928)

GIOVANNETTI

(1952)

THE DOG THAT DIDN'T.

VOILÀ LÉONIE! LA BONNE CANNE DES ANGLAIS!

MAIS OUI! REGARDEZ LE BANDEAU D'OR! C'EST TRÈS JOLI!!

RIDGEWELL

(1931)

(1954)

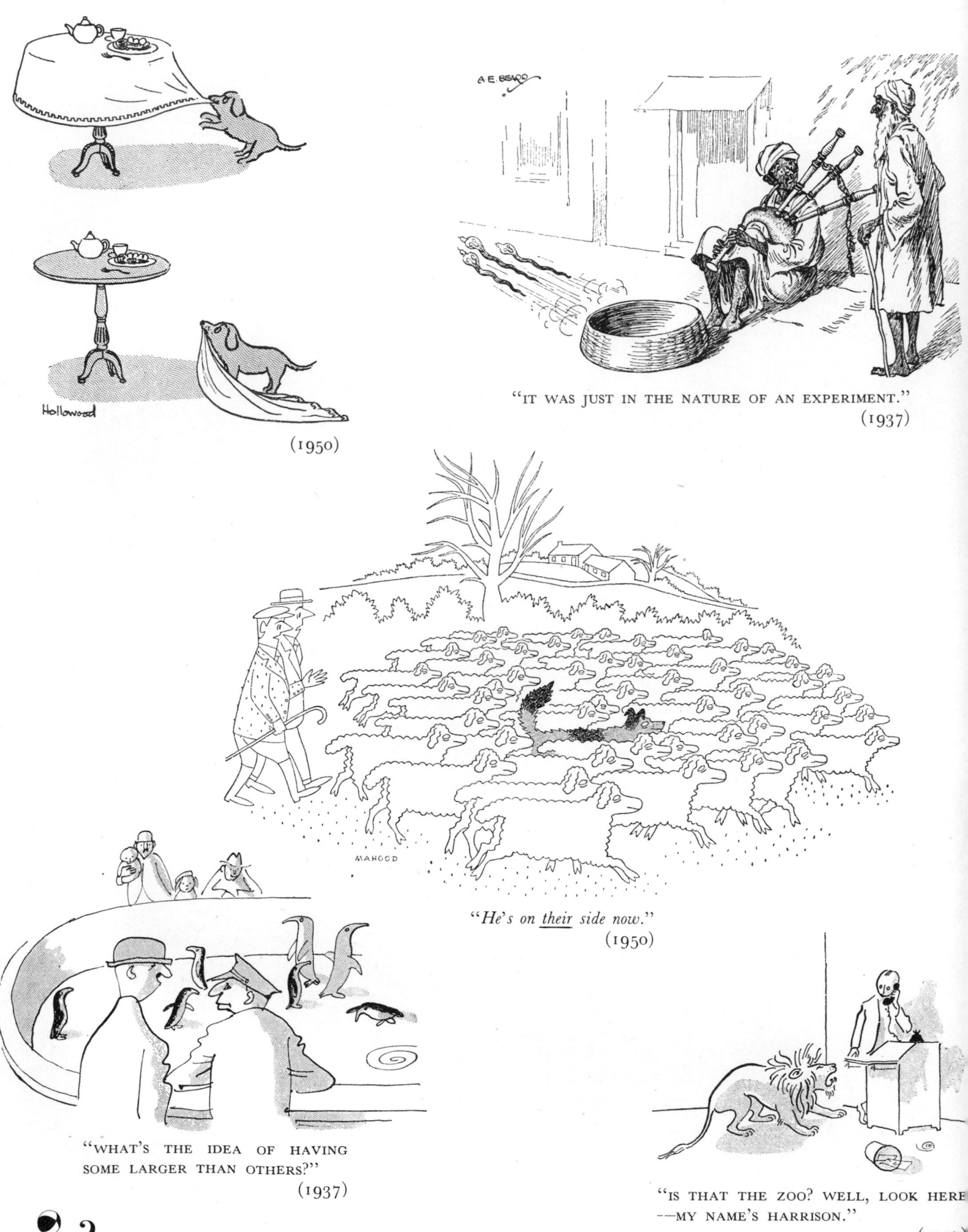

(1950)

"IT WAS JUST IN THE NATURE OF AN EXPERIMENT."
(1937)

"*He's on their side now.*"
(1950)

"WHAT'S THE IDEA OF HAVING SOME LARGER THAN OTHERS?"
(1937)

"IS THAT THE ZOO? WELL, LOOK HERE—MY NAME'S HARRISON."
(1937)

"OF COURSE I REALIZE THAT YOU FIND HER ATTRACTIVE, MY BOY, BUT DON'T FORGET THAT BEAUTY IS ONLY SKIN DEEP."

(1937)

"Darling — promise you'll never change.

(1949)

"I'M SO AFRAID THERE'S CRUELTY IN THEIR TRAINING."

(1936)

(1952)

"*That's what you get for being too darned intelligent.*"
(1946)

"*Darling!—he's playing our tune.*"
(1948)

"THE SECRET IS TO LOOK HIM STRAIGHT IN THE EYES."
(1937)

HAPPY THOUGHT! LET US ALL HAVE A VOICE IN THE MATTER.
Noble Breeder of Shorthorns: "WELL, YOU ARE A SPLENDID FELLOW, AND NO MISTAKE!"
Prize Bull: "SO WOULD YOU BE, MY LORD, IF YOU COULD ONLY HAVE CHOSEN YOUR PA AND MA AS CAREFULLY AND JUDICIOUSLY AS YOU CHOSE MINE!"
(1880)

"COME ON, YOU FOOL! HE'S NOT A CAMERAMAN."
(1934)

"Bad luck, Charlie. Mrs. Blaikie isn't coming out today."
(1949)

". . . now that's just what the act needed— some sort of climax."
(1948)

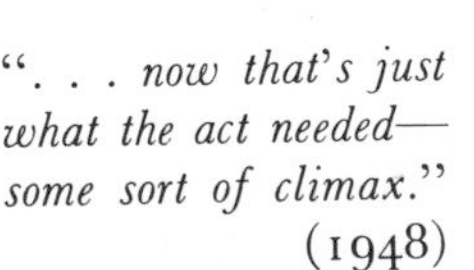

"Careful—that stung!"
(1947)

"I keep thinking it's Tuesday"

(1937)

"Stop criticizing" (1946)

"Sit" (1955)

(1955)

COUNTRY LIFE AND LEISURE

Hunting chaps may be disappointed with this section as it does not contain many hunting jokes. PUNCH was thick with hunting jokes in the Victorian era and this section is unrepresentative; but as stated in the preface, the purpose of this book is to amuse you today. The hunters that thundered through so many volumes were undoubtedly fleet and mettlesome, but the humour that accompanied them was heavy-footed.

THE FORCE OF HABIT
Whipper-in: "MASTER TOM HURT? BLESS YOU, NO, MUM! THE OLD MARE AND HIM NEVER MISSES THAT BROOK!"

(1867)

Contemplative man (in punt): "I DON'T SO MUCH CARE ABOUT THE SPORT, IT'S THE DELICIOUS REPOSE I ENJOY SO."

(1852)

NO CONSEQUENCE

"I SAY, JACK! WHO'S THAT COME TO GRIEF IN THE DITCH?"

"ONLY THE PARSON!"

"OH, LEAVE HIM THERE, THEN! HE WONT BE WANTED UNTIL NEXT SUNDAY!"

(1855)

WAGES AND WIVES

Philanthropic Farmer: "WELL, TOMKINS, AFTER THIS WEEK, INSTEAD OF PAYING YOU PARTLY IN CIDER, I SHALL GIVE YOU TWO SHILLINGS EXTRA WAGES."

Tomkins: "NO, THANKY', MASTER; THAT WON'T DO FOR ME!"

Farmer: "WHY, MAN, YOU'LL BE THE GAINER; FOR THE CIDER YOU HAD WASN'T WORTH TWO SHILLINGS!"

Tomkins: "AH, BUT YOU SEE I DRINKS THE CIDER MYSELF; BUT THE OW'D 'OOMAN 'LL 'EV THE TWO SHILLUN'!!"

(1872)

A CONSULTATION

Veterinary Surgeon: "LEGS QUEER, SIR! DO YOU 'ACK 'IM OR 'UNT 'IM?

Proprietor of Quadruped: "I HUNT HIM SOMETIMES, BUT I MOSTLY USE HIM AS A HACK."

Veterinary Surgeon: "AH, SIR, THAT'S WHERE IT IS. IT AIN'T THE 'UNTING AS 'URTS 'IM, IT'S THE 'AMMER, 'AMMER, 'AMMER ALONG THE 'ARD 'IGH ROAD!"

(1856)

NOT SO BAD AS HE SEEMS

Country Friend (*apropos of Cockney Ditto*): "UPON MY WORD, THOMAS, IF I HAD THOUGHT HE HAD BEEN SO DANGEROUS, I WOULDN'T HAVE BROUGHT HIM OUT."

Keeper: "WELL, HE DU SHOOT A LEETLE WILD, SIR—BUT IT AIN'T O' MUCH CONSEQUENCE—I LOAD FOR UN—AND I DON'T PUT NO SHOT IN!"

(1860)

POACHING v. PREACHING

Rector: "GOOD MORNING, MR. CATCHPOLE! I'M SORRY THAT I SEE YOU NOW SO SELDOM AT OUR SERVICES!"

Gamekeeper: "WELL, SIR, ALL I CAN SAY IS, IF THE N'IGHBORS KNOWED AS I WERE RIG'LAR AT THE CHU'CH, YOU'D BE 'NATION SURE TO LEWSE PRETTY NIGH HALF YAR CONGREGAITION!!"

(1871)

PHYSICAL GEOGRAPHY

English Angler (on this side of the Tweed): "HI, DONALD! COME OVER AND HELP ME TO LAND HIM—A 20-POUNDER I'LL SWEAR—"

Highlander (on the other): "IT WULL TAK' YE A LANG TIME TO LAN' THAT FUSH TOO, D'YE KEN, SIR, WHATEVER!—YE HAE HOOKED THE KINGDOM O' AULD SCOTLAND!"

(1881)

RURAL FELICITY

Sympathetic Old Parson: "YOU APPEAR IN DEEP THOUGHT, MY FRIEND. MAY I ASK WHAT CHIEFLY OCCUPIES YOUR MIND?"

Countryman: "MOSTLY NUTHIN'."

(1887)

Shepherd: "MON, SANDY, HE'S GOT NAE FLEE ON THE END O' THE LINE."

Sandy (sotto voce): "HAUD YER TONGUE, MON! HE DOES NO KEN, AND HE'S BETTER WITHOOT IT. HE WAS AYE CATCHIN' HISSELF AND ITHER TRASH!"

(1902)

Local Oracle: "WELL, GENTS, IT'S LIKE THIS 'ERE. THERE'S THINGS AS IS, AND THERE'S THINGS AS ISN'T; AND THERE'S SOME THINGS AS NEITHER IS NOR ISN'T. AND, TO MY THINKING, THIS 'ERE NOO REGULATION O' THE PARISH COUNCIL COMES SOMEWHERE BETWEEN THE LAST TWO."

(1908)

"I AM SO GLAD TO SEE YOU ABOUT AGAIN AFTER YOUR LONG ILLNESS, JAKES."

"THANKEE, MARM, THANKEE! BUT I BE THAT OLD, 'TWARN'T 'ARDLY WUTH THE TROUBLE O' GETTIN' WELL."

(1902)

HE KNEW HIS WORK

Proprietor of Travelling Menagerie: "ARE YOU USED TO LOOKING AFTER HORSES AND OTHER ANIMALS?"

Applicant for Job: "YESSIR. BEEN USED TO 'ORSES ALL MY LIFE."

P.O.T.M.: "WHAT STEPS WOULD YOU TAKE IF A LION GOT LOOSE?"

A.F.J.: "GOOD LONG UNS, MISTER!"

(1905)

AFTER THE RACES

Little 'Arry (who has had a "bad day"—to driver of public coach): "EVER LOSE ANY MONEY BACKIN' 'ORSES, COACHIE?"

Driver: "NOT 'ALF! LOST TWENTY QUID ONCE—BACKED A PAIR OF 'ORSES AND A HOMNIBUS INTO A WINDOW IN REGENT STREET!"

(1906)

Modest but unsuccessful tyro (who has been flogging the river for hours): "IS THERE ANYTHING I AM OMITTING TO DO, MCWHIRR?"
McW.: "I WADNA JUST SAY THAT EXACTLY. BUT I'M THINKIN' YE DRINK VARRA LEETLE WHUSKY FOR A MAN WHAE'S NO KILLIN' FUSH."

(1908)

The New Pupil: "DO I WAKE HIM UP OR MILK HIM WHERE HE IS?"

(1930)

The Pupil: "WHAT DO I DO NOW I'VE FINISHED WINDING?"
The Instructor: "CLIMB UP THE ROD AND STAB IT."

(1923)

"IT'S WONDERFUL WHAT THE HAND OF MAN CAN DO TO A PIECE OF EARTH, WITH THE AID OF DIVINE PROVIDENCE, WILKS."
"YOU SHOULD 'AVE SEEN THIS PIECE, SIR, WHEN DIVINE PROVIDENCE 'AD IT ALL TO ITSELF."

(1934)

Motorist: "WILL THIS ROAD TAKE ME TO HONITON?"
Boy: "I DOAN'T KNOW."
Motorist: "DOES IT GO THROUGH CHARD?"
Boy: "I DOAN'T KNOW."
Motorist: "YOU DON'T SEEM TO KNOW MUCH, DO YOU?"
Boy: "NOA—BUT I BAIN'T LOST!"

(1930)

Hostess: "W-WHAT'S HAPPENED?"
Colonel (*fiercely*): "I RETURNED HIS FIRE."

(1935)

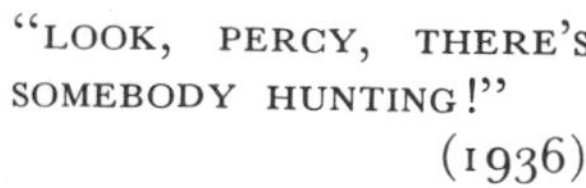

"LOOK, PERCY, THERE'S SOMEBODY HUNTING!"

(1936)

SINGULAR PHENOMENON IN THE HUNTING-FIELD

WHY IS IT THE JOY OF FOLLOWING HOUNDS

SEEMS TO VARY

IN INVERSE PROPORTION

TO THE FINANCIAL STATUS OF THE PARTICIPANT IN THE HUNT?

(1936)

(1954)

(1938)

"*Ah! here comes the farmer—grumbling as usual, I'll be bound.*"

(1947)

Voice from Within: "IS THAT YOU, MR. PETTIGREW? THANK YOU SO MUCH. LEAVE THE MILK OUTSIDE."

(1933)

A WEEK-END AT AN IDEAL COTTAGE

THE IDEAL COTTAGE

THE STRENUOUS OWNERS

THE DOMESTIC STAFF

THE GUEST

THE FLIGHT FROM TOWN

THE DRIVE FROM THE STATION

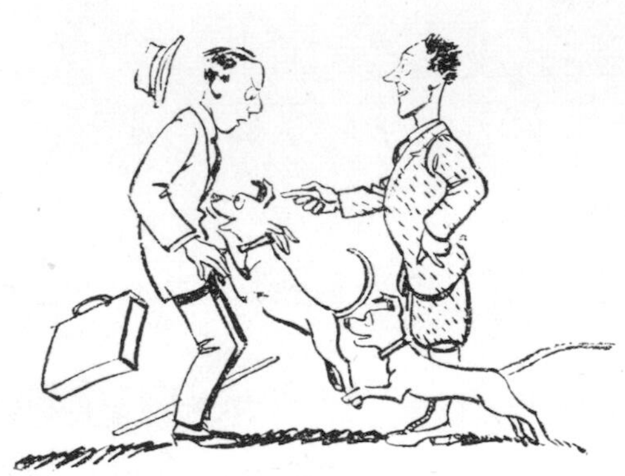

THE WARM WELCOME—

THE NON-ALCOHOLIC DRINK

THE FUNNY FEELING AFTERWARDS

THE JOLLY TUNES

THE EARLY RETIREMENT

THE GUEST CHAMBER

(1923)

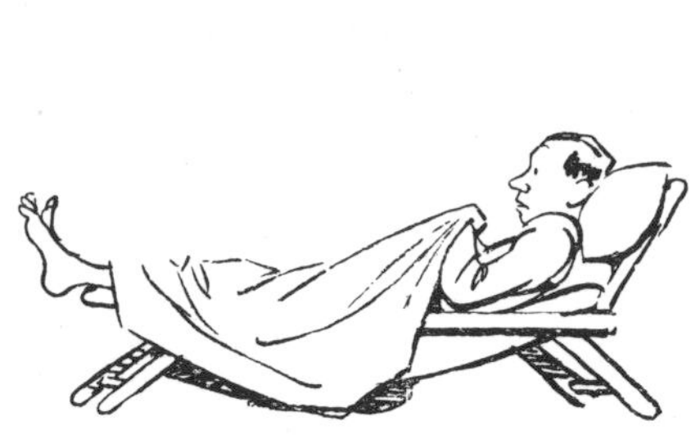

THE SNUG LITTLE BED

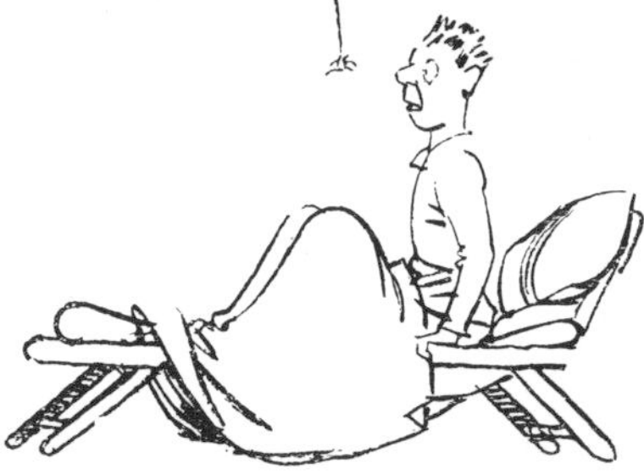

THE SOCIABLE SPIDER

THE BUSY RATS

THE EARLY-MORNING SOUNDS

THE BATH IN THE BASIN

THE HEALTHY PORRIDGE

THE TWELVE-MILE WALK—

ACROSS COUNTRY

THE RETURN HOME

THE SUDDENLY-REMEMBERED APPOINTMENT

Arthur Watts (1923)

THE FLIGHT TO TOWN

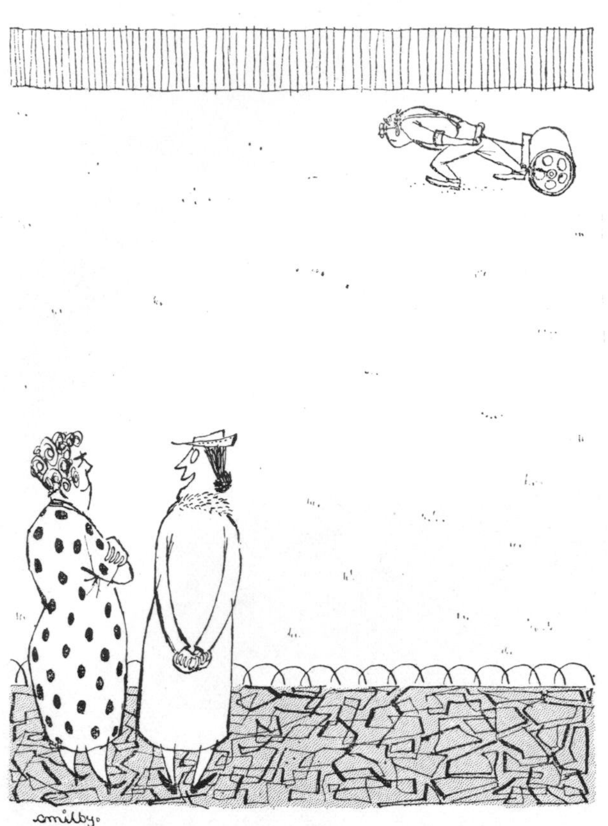

"I didn't know your husband was keen on gardening."
(1952)

"I am cutting the grass." (1952)

THE BRITISH CHARACTER
ENTHUSIASM FOR HUNTING

(1936)

"HAROLD, LOOK! ISN'T THAT SWEET? HE'S PICKED A TULIP."

(1933)

"CONGRATULATIONS, LADY PAMELA. YOU HAVE BAGGED YOUR FIRST LION!"

(1933)

"That's wheat!!!"
(1954)

THE BRITISH CHARACTER
EXTRAORDINARY PROPENSITY OF FARMERS TO GRUMBLE
(1936)

Increasing mechanization of the countryside is enabling more and more people to afford the luxury of owning . . .

. . . a horse.

(1956)

"I'm afraid I won't be able to sit to-day."

(1955)

(1953)

thelwell

BOTH SIDES OF THE COUNTER

Shopman: "IT'S MY OWN INVENTION, AND WARRANTED TO PRODUCE A LUXURIANT CROP OF CURLS ON THE BALDEST HEAD WITHIN FOUR-AND-TWENTY HOURS."

(1846)

Fair Customer: "IS THIS COLOUR FAST AND REALLY GENUINE?"

Gallant Shop Assistant: "AS GENUINE AS THE ROSES ON YOUR CHEEKS, MADAM."

Fair Customer: "H'M—ER—SHOW ME SOMETHING ELSE."

(1908)

TURNING HIS FLANK

Mr. Brisket (the Butcher): "GOOD MORNING, MR. CHATTLES! YOU'RE A LAWYER, AND I WANT YOUR ADVICE. WHAT CAN I DO WITH A MAN WHOSE DOG STEALS SOME MEAT FROM MY SHOP?"

Mr. Chattles (the Lawyer): "DEMAND THE VALUE, OR SUMMON THE OWNER."

Mr. Brisket (triumphantly): "THEN I WANT SIX-AND-SIXPENCE FROM YOU, SIR, OR ELSE I'LL SUMMONS YER! YOUR DOG THERE RAN AWAY WITH A PIECE OF MUTTON O' THAT VALUE FROM THESE PREMISES LAST NIGHT!"

Mr. Chattles: "HUM—AH—H'M! THEN IF YOU'LL HAND ME OVER TWOPENCE, WE SHALL JUST BE SQUARE, MR. BRISKET— AS MY FEE FOR CONSULTATION IS SIX-AND-EIGHTPENCE!"

(1879)

SCENE—*High-class outfitter's in Bond Street*
Elegant Assistant (suavely): "AND WHAT IS YOUR PLEASURE, SIR?"
Country Squire (pondering for a moment): "ER — FOX-HUNTING, CHIEFLY; BUT WHAT I WANT NOW IS A HAT."

(1925)

THE CHRISTMAS SHOPPING

Shopwalker: "ANYTHING ELSE WE CAN HAVE THE PLEASURE OF SHOWING YOU, MADAM?"
Paterfamilias: "THE DOOR!"

(1898)

"IN ANY CASE, MR. SMITH, WAIT UNTIL HE WAKES NATURALLY. IT'S JUST POSSIBLE IT'S ONE OF THE DIRECTORS."

(1934)

GET YOUR SURPRISE GIFT FROM SANTA CLAUS

HOSIERY

TOILET REQUISITES

BE-ROP ✱ BAGS

HUB·UB PERFUME

COMPLAINTS

MAHOOD

(1950)

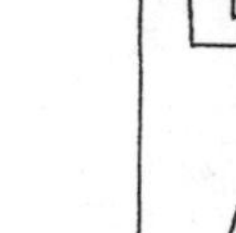

(1938)

"MY WIFE BOUGHT THIS JUMPER HERE LAST WEEK. NOW SHE WANTS ANOTHER LIKE IT."
"YES, SIR. WHAT BUST?"
"OH, NOTHING—SHE TORE IT ON A NAIL."

(1933)

"I'M CHOOSING A HAT AS A SURPRISE GIFT TO MY SISTER-IN-LAW AND MY HUSBAND HAS THE FAMILY FEATURES IN A MARKED DEGREE."

(1935)

Manager of Drapery Stores: "WHAT DO YOU MEAN BY ARGUING WITH THAT LADY? LET HER HAVE HER OWN WAY. REMEMBER, A CUSTOMER IS ALWAYS RIGHT."
Assistant: "BUT SHE SAID WE WERE SWINDLERS."

(1923)

"It's only fair to tell Madam that the parfumiers are frankly unable to set limits to the seductive powers of this one or to calculate in advance what its main effects will be."

(1954)

(1952)

"If business doesn't buck up soon we shall have to look for larger premises."

(1953)

"*How shall I break all these to my husband?*"
(1952)

"*Because I dislike shaving.*"
(1952)

"*How many more of these Information jokes are we going to see?*"
(1952)

ENTERTAINMENT WORLDS

In the early days, the PUNCH Staff were devoted to the Theatre and their own amateur theatricals. Future Editor-in-chief Francis Burnand wrote *Cox and Box* (music by Sullivan) and George du Maurier acted in it. Editor-in-chief Mark Lemon and John Leech were to be found acting in a farce with Charles Dickens. At times all the PUNCH Staff were pressed into acting service. How strange then that their hobby threw up no jokes that have lasted.

The prophecy of television (p. 72) was as a practical convenience rather than as an entertainment medium and godsend to the humorous artist.

In this section is the only joke in PUNCH that took four pages and fifty-eight drawings in its telling.

(1954)

Leading Man in Travelling Company: "WE PLAY HAMLET TONIGHT, LADDIE, DO WE NOT?"
Sub-Manager: "YES, MR. MONTGOMERY."
Leading Man: "THEN I MUST BORROW THE SUM OF TWO-PENCE."
Sub-Manager: "WHY?"
Leading Man: "I HAVE FOUR DAYS' GROWTH UPON MY CHIN. ONE CANNOT PLAY HAMLET IN A BEARD!"
Sub-Manager: "UM—WELL—WE'LL PUT ON MACBETH!"

(1912)

He: "ARE WE ALONE?"
Voice from the Gallery: "NO, GUV'NOR; BUT YOU WILL BE TOMORROW NIGHT!"

(1906)

SCENE—A Boarding-house
Wife: "WHY DO YOU ALWAYS SIT AT THE PIANO, DAVID? YOU KNOW YOU CAN'T PLAY A NOTE!"
David: "NEITHER CAN ANYONE ELSE, WHILE I AM HERE!"

(1906)

"IS YOUR SON IMPROVING IN HIS VIOLIN PLAYING, MR. JONES?"
"WELL—EITHER HE'S IMPROVING, OR WE'RE GETTING USED TO IT."

(1895)

"PARDON ME, MADAM, BUT DO YOU MIND REPLACING YOUR HAT? I CAN'T SEE."

"THANK YOU."

(1924)

Chairman (proposing toast of the performers): "ALL THE HARTISTS HAVE GIVE THEIR SERVICES FREE, AND I THINK YOU'LL AGREE WITH ME, GENTLEMEN, THAT THE LABOURERS ARE WORTHY OF THEIR HIRE."

(1914)

AN ENGLISH NOBLEMAN AS A RULE DOES NOT ACT IN THE ABOVE MANNER DURING A MISUNDERSTANDING WITH A LADY WHO HAS ENGAGED HIS AFFECTIONS.

ENGLISH SPORTSMEN AND SPORTS-WOMEN ARE SELDOM AS DECORATIVE AS THIS.

WHEN THE NOTICE PRECEDING THE PICTURE DEFINITELY STATES THAT THE ACTION TAKES PLACE IN PICCADILLY THE ABOVE DOESN'T LOOK RIGHT SOMEHOW.

(1913)

HINTS TO FOREIGNERS WHO PRODUCE CINEMA FILMS FOR THE ENGLISH MARKET

EDISON'S TELEPHONOSCOPE

Paterfamilias (in Wilton Place): "BEATRICE, COME CLOSER, I WANT TO WHISPER."
Beatrice (from Ceylon): "YES, PAPA DEAR."
Paterfamilias: "WHO IS THAT CHARMING YOUNG LADY PLAYING ON CHARLIE'S SIDE?"
Beatrice: "SHE'S JUST COME OVER FROM ENGLAND, PAPA. I'LL INTRODUCE YOU TO HER AS SOON AS THE GAME'S OVER."

(1878)

DEVELOPMENT OF WIRELESS TELEGRAPHY. SCENE IN HYDE PARK.

(*These two figures are not communicating with one another. The lady is receiving an amatory message, and the gentleman some racing results.*)

(1906)

Visitor: "HOW NICE FOR HIM! NOW HE CAN LISTEN TO ALL THE BEST MUSIC."
Fond Mother: "YES—AND IT'S SO GOOD FOR HIS EARS—THEY DID STICK OUT SO."

(1923)

"WHY CAN'T YOU REMEMBER TO TURN THE WIRELESS OFF WHEN YOU LEAVE THE CAR, HENRY?"

(1933)

YOUR FIRST WIRELESS SET

WHEN YOU HAVE YOUR FIRST WIRELESS SET INSTALLED FOR YOU—

Fougasse

DO NOT DELAY—

TO TAKE FULL ADVANTAGE—

OF ITS ENTERTAINMENT—

FOR ONCE—

YOU GET—

BITTEN—

WITH THE SUBJECT—

YOU WILL—

NEVER AGAIN—

HAVE—

MUCH—

LEISURE FOR LISTENING.

(1952)

"How much is this one?"

(1954)

"Of course, in the book, they never actually meet."
(1951)

"Inform the new signwriter I want a word with him in my office."
(1949)

"Wait a minute—what's this going to be like on the wide screen?"
(1954)

(1954)

(1955)

HERO WORSHIP: DISTRACTIONS OF THE FILM WORLD
(1920)

"We're rather worried about William."

(1954)

(1950)

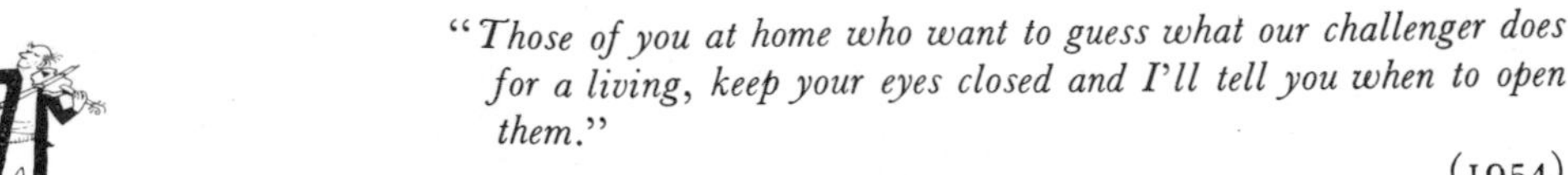

"Those of you at home who want to guess what our challenger does for a living, keep your eyes closed and I'll tell you when to open them."

(1954)

(1949)

(1954)

(1954)

[SEE OVER

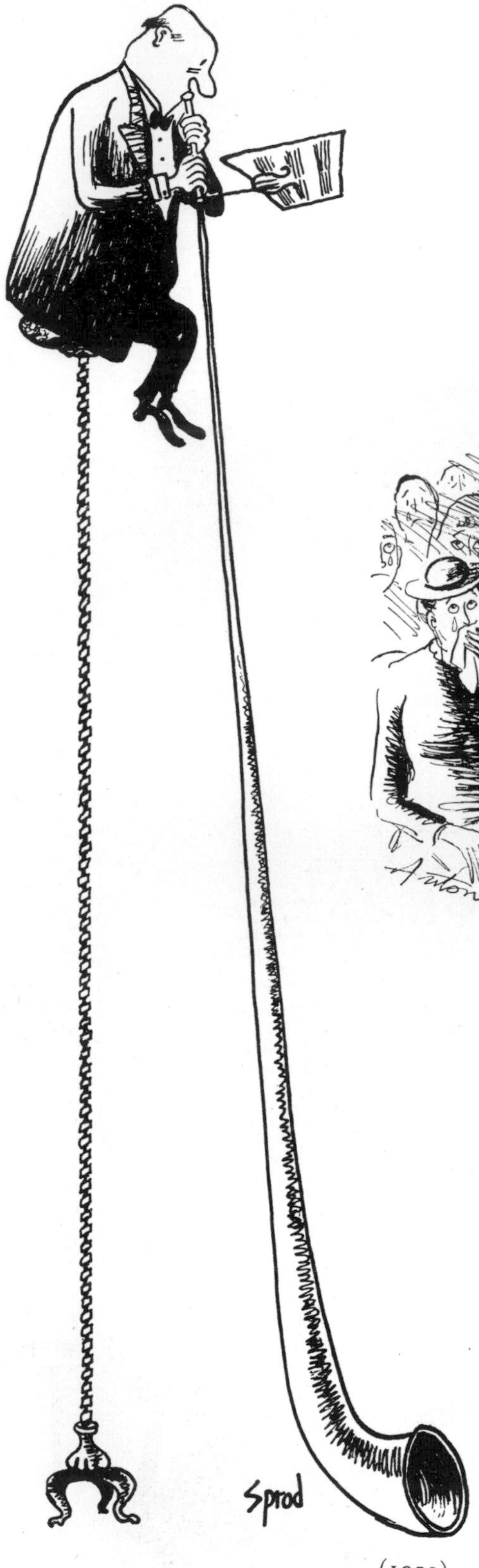

(1950)

"Henry—you've forgotten your glasses again."

(1952)

THE ONE-NOTE MAN

MORE TO COME!

PRESS ON!

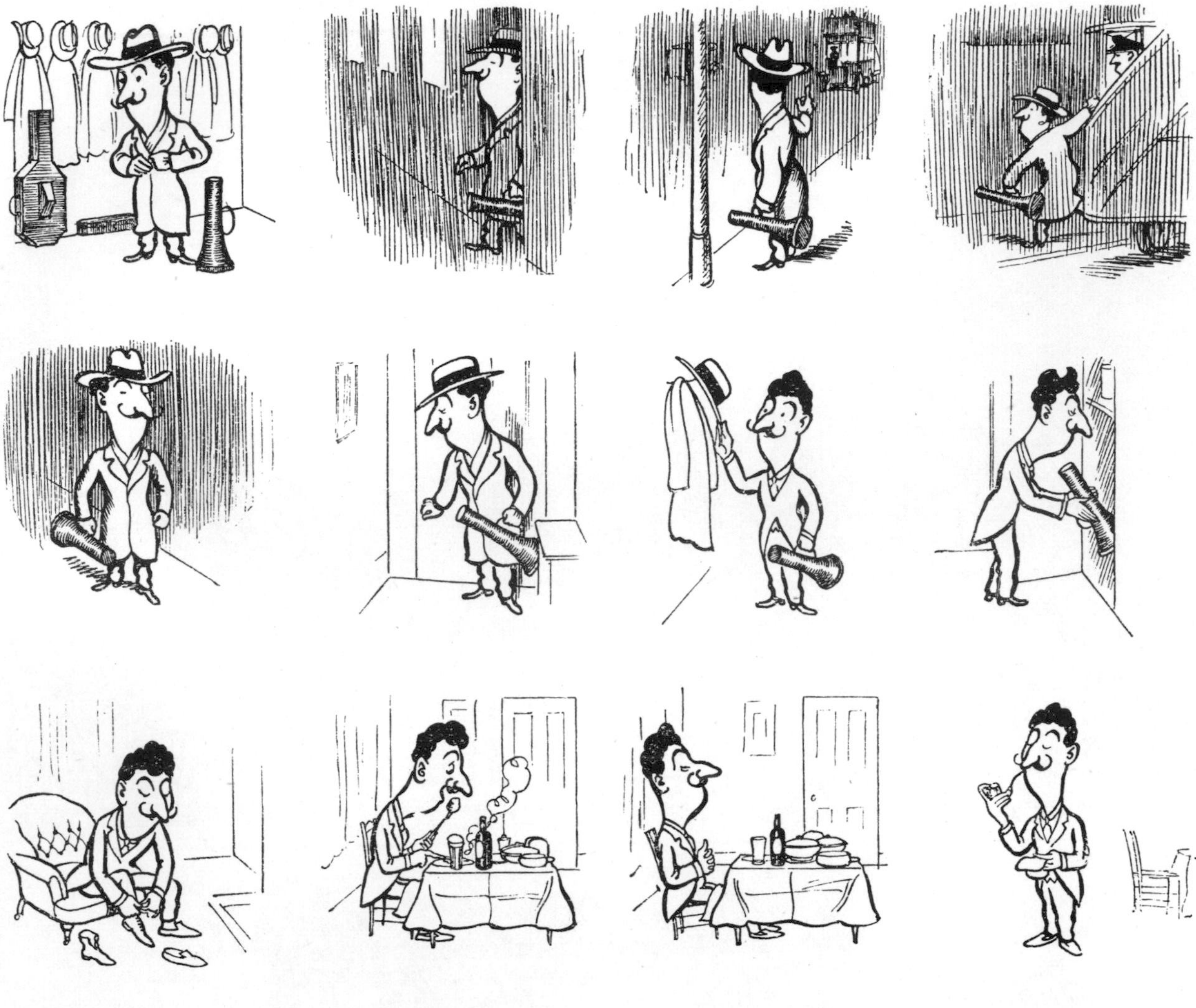

(1921)

THE BRITISH CHARACTER

LOVE OF ARRIVING LATE AT THEATRICAL PRODUCTIONS

(1936)

THE BRITISH CHARACTER

FAILURE TO APPRECIATE GOOD MUSIC

(1934)

(1955)

(1948)

(1948)

LOVE, COURTSHIP . . . AND IT TAKES TWO!

PUNCH was committed to an attitude of cynicism by the fantastic popularity of a one-line fill-in in an 1845 issue:

"ADVICE TO PERSONS ABOUT TO MARRY—DON'T"

It is still quoted widely today.

Luckily this advice has been even more widely disregarded than it has been quoted, otherwise this section would be a sorry one.

"That's all—you can stop smiling now." (1948)

A PERFECT WRETCH

Wife: "WHY, DEAR ME, WILLIAM; HOW TIME FLIES! I DECLARE WE HAVE BEEN MARRIED TEN YEARS TODAY!"

Wretch: "HAVE WE, LOVE? I AM SURE I THOUGHT IT HAD BEEN A GREAT DEAL LONGER."

(1851)

MALICIOUS

Flora: "CAN YOU STILL SEE THE STEAMER, LUCY DEAR?"

Lucy: "OH YES, QUITE PLAINLY!"

Flora: "AND DEAR, DEAR WILLIAM, TOO?"

Lucy: "OH, YES!"

Flora: "DOES HE SEEM UNHAPPY, NOW HE IS AWAY FROM ME?"

Lucy: "EVIDENTLY, I SHOULD SAY, DEAR; FOR HE IS SMOKING A CIGAR, AND DRINKING SOMETHING OUT OF A TUMBLER TO CHEER HIM, POOR FELLOW."

(1857)

Affectionate Husband: "COME, POLLY—IF I AM A LITTLE IRRITABLE, IT'S OVER IN A MINUTE!!"

(1847)

"MAMMA, SHALL YOU LET ME GO TO THE WILKINSONS' BALL, IF THEY GIVE ONE, THIS WINTER?"
"NO, DARLING!" (*A pause.*)
"YOU'VE BEEN TO A GREAT MANY BALLS, HAVEN'T YOU, MAMMA?"
"YES, DARLING,—AND I'VE SEEN THE FOLLY OF THEM ALL." (*Another pause.*)
"MIGHTN'T I JUST SEE THE FOLLY OF ONE, MAMMA?" (*A very long pause.*)

(1874)

A LITTLE FAMILY BREEZE
Mrs. T.: "WHAT A WRETCH YOU MUST BE, T.; WHY DON'T YOU TAKE ME OFF? DON'T YOU SEE I'M OVERTOOK WITH THE TIDE, AND I SHALL BE DROWNDED!"
T.: "WELL, THEN—WILL YOU PROMISE NOT TO KICK UP SUCH A ROW WHEN I STOP OUT LATE OF A SATURDAY?"

(1864)

Lady: "SUCH A BEAUTIFUL CREATURE MUST BE GOOD-TEMPERED!"
Husband: "JUST WHAT I THOUGHT WHEN I MARRIED YOU, MY DEAR."

(1875)

NATURAL RELIGION

Bishop (reproving delinquent Page): "WRETCHED BOY! WHO IS IT THAT SEES AND HEARS ALL WE DO, AND BEFORE WHOM EVEN I AM BUT AS A CRUSHED WORM?"

Page: "THE MISSUS, MY LORD!"

(1880)

First Stranger: "I DECLARE, SIR, THAT WOMEN ARE GETTING MORE OUTRAGEOUSLY DECOLLETÉ EVERY DAY. JUST LOOK OVER THERE, AT THAT PRODIGIOUS OLD PORPOISE WITH THE EYEGLASS!"

Second Stranger: "HUM! HA! YES! I CAN'T HELP THINKING SHE'S A MORE FESTIVE-LOOKING OBJECT THAN THAT FUNEREAL OLD FRUMP WITH THE FAN!"

First Stranger: "THE 'FUNEREAL OLD FRUMP' IS MY WIFE, SIR!"

Second Stranger: "THE 'PRODIGIOUS OLD PORPOISE' IS MINE! LET'S GO AND HAVE SOME TEA!"

(1872)

A DISENCHANTMENT

Grandpapa: "WHAT? BOB IN LOVE WITH MISS FONTALBA, THE COMIC ACTRESS AT THE PARTHENON?"

Bob (firing up): "YES, GRANDPA! AND IF YOU'VE GOT A WORD TO SAY AGAINST THAT LADY, IT HAD BETTER NOT BE SAID IN MY PRESENCE, THAT'S ALL!"

Grandpapa: "I SAY A WORD AGAINST HER! WHY, BLESS YOUR HEART, MY DEAR BOY! I WAS HEAD OVER EARS IN LOVE WITH HER MYSELF—WHEN I WAS YOUR AGE!"

(1884)

THE WANING OF THE HONEYMOON

Angelina (suppressing an inclination to yawn): "HOW NICE IT WOULD BE IF SOME FRIEND WERE TO TURN UP; WOULDN'T IT, EDWIN?"

Edwin (after yawning elaborately): "YE-E-ES! — OR EVEN SOME ENEMY!"

(1878)

Wife: "POOR MAMMA IS DREADFULLY LOW-SPIRITED THIS MORNING, GEORGE. ONLY THINK—SHE HAS JUST EXPRESSED A WISH TO BE CREMATED!"
Husband (with alacrity): "'O'B-LESS MY—" (*Throwing down his Newspaper.*) "TELL HER TO PUT HER THINGS ON, DEAR! I'LL—I'LL DRIVE HER OVER AT ONCE!!"

(1888)

Small Voice from under the Bed: "NO, I WILL NOT COME OUT! I TELL YOU, ONCE AND FOR ALL, BERNESIA, I WILL BE MASTER IN MY OWN HOUSE!"

(1896)

Fair Bride of Nineteen Summers: "WHAT CAN THEY ALL SEE IN HER? I'M SURE SHE'S OVER THIRTY; AND NO WOMAN IS WORTH LOOKING AT AFTER THAT!"
Matron (age unknown): "NOR WORTH SPEAKING TO BEFORE, MY DEAR!"

(1882)

The Colonel: "YES; HE WAS SENIOR WRANGLER OF HIS YEAR, AND SHE TOOK A MATHEMATICAL SCHOLARSHIP AT GIRTON; AND NOW THEY'RE ENGAGED!"
Mrs. Jones: "DEAR ME, HOW INTERESTING! AND OH, HOW DIFFERENT THEIR CONVERSATION MUST BE FROM THE INSIPID TWADDLE OF ORDINARY LOVERS!"

THEIR CONVERSATION

He: "AND WHAT WOULD DOVEY DO, IF LOVEY WERE TO DIE?"
She: "OH, DOVEY WOULD DIE TOO!"

(1884)

Stern Voice (*from first-floor landing,* 12:10 *A.M.*): "ALICE!"
Alice (*softly*): "YES, 'PA!"
Voice (*with a threatening ring in it*): "DOES THAT YOUNG MAN IN THE FRONT PARLOUR TAKE TEA OR COFFEE FOR HIS BREAKF—!!" ("*Door*"! —*and he was gone!*)

(1889)

EMANCIPATION

Young Bride of Three Hours' Standing (*just starting on her Wedding Trip*): "OH, EDWIN DEAR! HERE'S TOM JONES. PAPA TOLD ME I WASN'T TO READ IT TILL I WAS MARRIED! THE DAY HAS COME . . . . AT LAST! BUY IT FOR ME, EDWIN DEAR."

(1891)

FOND AND FOOLISH

Edwin (*suddenly, after a long pause*): "DARLING!"
Angelina: "YES, DARLING?"
Edwin: "NOTHING, DARLING. ONLY DARLING, DARLING!"
(*Bilious Old Gentleman feels quite sick.*)

(1

"BE IT TRUE AS YOUR NEVVY B'AIN'T A-GOIN' TO MARRY THAT MISS GILES AFTER ALL?"
"WELL, YOU SEE, I 'VISED 'UN TO GIE UP MATRIMONY, AN' TAKE TO A TRADE."
(1898)

"JUST LOOK AT MR. JONES OVER THERE, FLIRTING WITH THAT GIRL! I ALWAYS THOUGHT HE WAS A WOMAN-HATER!"
"SO HE IS; BUT SHE'S NOT HERE TONIGHT!"
(1895)

Ethel: "WHY, WHAT'S THE MATTER, GERTRUDE?"
Gertrude: "OH, NOTHING. ONLY JACK AND I HAD A QUARREL THE OTHER DAY, AND I WROTE AND TOLD HIM NEVER TO DARE TO SPEAK OR WRITE TO ME AGAIN,—AND THE WRETCH HASN'T EVEN HAD THE DECENCY TO ANSWER MY LETTER!"
(1898)

First Young Wife: "DO YOU FIND IT MORE ECONOMICAL, DEAR, TO DO YOUR OWN COOKING?"
Second Young Wife: "OH, CERTAINLY. MY HUSBAND DOESN'T EAT HALF SO MUCH AS HE DID!"
(1901)

He (*with pride*): "YES, DEAR, MY FATHER AND MOTHER LIVED TOGETHER FOR FORTY WHOLE YEARS, AND NEVER HAD A SINGLE QUARREL!"
His Bride: "HOW TERRIBLY MONOTONOUS, DARLING!"

(1900)

"Twenty-five years' married life and never a quarrel! I always said you were spineless."

(1952)

A:. "THAT'S JONES'S DAUGHTER WITH HIM. SHE'S JUST ABOUT TO BE MARRIED."
B.: "WHO'S THE LUCKY MAN?"
A.: "JONES."

(1903)

Lady: "GENERALLY SPEAKING, WOMEN ARE—
Nasty Man (*interrupting*): "YES, THEY ARE."
Lady: "ARE WHAT?"
Nasty Man: "GENERALLY SPEAKING."

(1903)

Kind Friend: "PARDON ME, BUT I OUGHT TO TELL YOU THAT JONES HAS RUN AWAY WITH YOUR WIFE."
Husband (bored): "BUT WHY RUN?"

(1905)

Son: "MUVVER, TELL ME 'OW FARVER GOT TER KNOW YER."
Mother: "ONE DYE I FELL INTO THE WATER AN' 'E JUMPED IN AN' FISHED ME AHT."
Son (thoughtfully): "H'M, THET'S FUNNY; 'E WON'T LET ME LEARN TER SWIM."

(1920)

UNDER RESERVE

He: "DARLING, WILL YOU SHARE MY LOT?"
She: "YES, CHARLIE, IF IT REALLY IS A LOT."

(1905)

CLUB REGULATIONS

Female Voice (on telephone): "IS THAT THE HALL PORTER? WELL, I WANT TO KNOW IF YOU CAN GIVE A MESSAGE TO MY HUSBAND."
Hall Porter: "I AM SORRY, MADAM, BUT YOUR HUSBAND IS NOT IN THE CLUB."
Female Voice: "BUT I HAVE NOT TOLD YOU MY HUSBAND'S NAME YET "
Hall Porter: "QUITE UNNECESSARY, MADAM. NOBODY'S HUSBAND IS EVER HERE BY ANY CHANCE."

(1912)

Newly-Affianced Young Lady (who is never going to forget the dance she has just had): "CAN YOU TELL ME THE NAME OF THAT LOVELY TUNE YOU JUST PLAYED?"
Member of Orchestra: "CERTAINLY. IT'S CALLED 'I DO LIKE MY LITTLE DROP OF BEER.'"

(1928)

Proud Father: "THE MAN WHO MARRIES MY DAUGHTER, SIR, WINS A PRIZE."
Young Man: "BY JOVE! THAT'S A GREAT IDEA. IS IT A MONEY PRIZE OR JUST A SILVER CUP?"

(1927)

Clergyman: "WILT THOU HAVE THIS WOMAN TO THY WEDDED WIFE?"
Bride (grimly): "HE WILL."

(1924)

Groomsman: "ARE YOU A FRIEND OF THE BRIDE OR BRIDEGROOM, SIR?"
Testy Old Gentleman: "I DISLIKE THEM BOTH INTENSELY."

(1925)

WHERE IGNORANCE IS BLISS

(1928)

"BUT OF COURSE SOMEBODY ELSE WILL HAVE TO BE PRIME MINISTER WHILE HE'S SWIMMING THE CHANNEL."

(1937)

Counsel: "THE CROSS-EXAMINATION DID NOT SEEM TO WORRY YOU AT ALL. HAVE YOU HAD ANY PREVIOUS EXPERIENCE?"
Client: "THREE WIVES."

(1922)

Wife: "YOU SEEM UPSET, MY DEAR."
Husband: "JUST COME UP IN THE TRAIN WITH THAT FELLOW TUBBARD. HE'S ALWAYS COMPLAINING THAT HIS WIFE SEEMS TO BE GROWING SO OLD; DASHED BAD FORM, I THINK. COULDN'T STICK IT ANY LONGER, AND TOLD HIM STRAIGHT OUT, I ALWAYS SAW YOU AS YOU USED TO BE, THANK GOD!"

(1928)

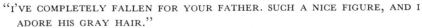

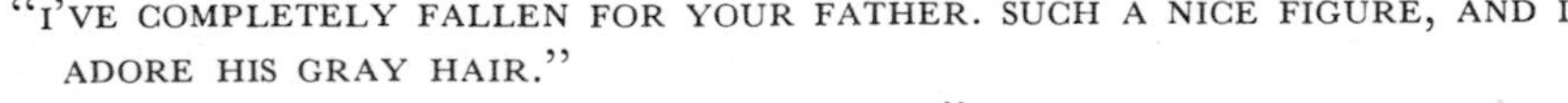
"I'VE COMPLETELY FALLEN FOR YOUR FATHER. SUCH A NICE FIGURE, AND I ADORE HIS GRAY HAIR."
"SO GLAD, DARLING. THE HAIR IS MY DOING."

(1929)

ROMANCE

MONICA HAD OFTEN ADMIRED THOSE MAGAZINE ILLUSTRATIONS—

PICTURING— GALLANT RESCUES— DURING THE BATHING SEASON;

BUT IT WAS QUITE DIFFERENT WHEN IT HAPPENED TO MONICA.

(1928)

"WELL, I SHALL GIVE HER ANOTHER HALF-HOUR AND THEN I'M THROUGH WITH WOMEN."

(1934)

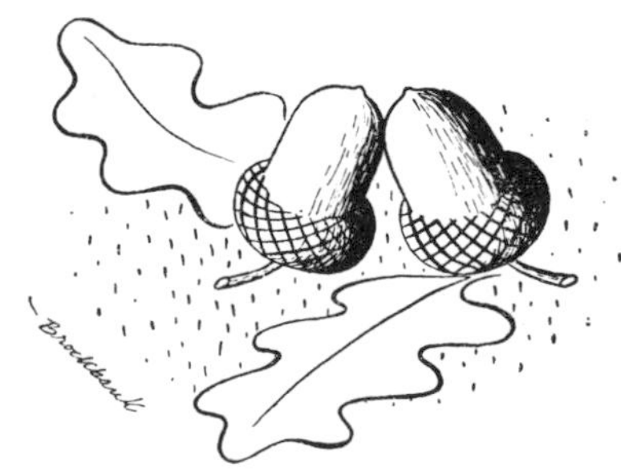

"Confidentially, my dear, I think I'm going to have an oak."

(1939)

Young Bride: "OH, LOOK, DARLING, OUR FIRST BILLS!"

(1929)

Mistress (sternly): "ARE YOU AWARE THE MASTER HAD TO GO TO TOWN WITHOUT HIS BREAKFAST?"
Maid: "WE HEARD THE DOOR SLAM. WE THOUGHT YOU'D LEFT HIM."

(1930)

She: "ADAM, THE FIRST GARDENER HAD A WIFE, DONALD, AND SO SHOULD YOU."
Donald: "AY, MISS, HE DID; AND HOW LONG DID HE KEEP HIS JOB AFTER THAT?"

(1933)

(1933)

Wife (bitterly): "LOOK AT 'IM! AND THEN 'EAR WHAT 'E SAYS WHEN I ASK 'IM TO GIVE A 'AND WITH THE CHILD'S PRAM!"

(1931)

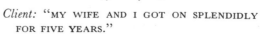

Client: "MY WIFE AND I GOT ON SPLENDIDLY FOR FIVE YEARS."
Solicitor: "AH! WHAT HAPPENED THEN?"
Client: "SHE CAME BACK."

(1928)

A SPOT OF BOTHER

IT'S EASY ENOUGH TO GET UP FROM THE TABLE—

MAKE FOR THE DOOR—

TURN ROUND AND HAVE THE LAST WORD—

STORM OUT—

AND BANG THE DOOR VIOLENTLY AFTER YOU—

BUT IT'S SO AWKWARD WHEN YOU HAPPEN TO HAVE LEFT YOUR PIPE ON THE MANTELPIECE!

(1933)

Wife: "MIND YOU, DEARIE, 'E AIN'T 'ANDSOME, BUT 'IS FACE DOES IMPROVE WHEN YOU GET IT BETWEEN A CLEAN COLLAR AN' A NEW 'AT."
(1934)

"*Hurry up, Alice. Father's dropping little hints about being kept waiting.*"
(1939)

"YOU'LL BE SURPRISED TO KNOW, SIR, THAT I'M IN LOVE WITH YOUR DAUGHTER—IN FACT I CAN THINK OF NOTHING ELSE."
(1937)

"AND HERE'S ONE OF HIM TAKEN AT EASTBOURNE WHEN HE WAS FIVE."
(1938)

"Well, I'll marry you if you insist—but who do you suppose you're speaking to?"

(1947)

(1948)

THE BRITISH CHARACTER

A TENDENCY TO LEAVE THE WASHING-UP TILL LATER

(1938)

"I THOUGHT I'D KEEP IT ON TILL YOU WERE PLEASED TO NOTICE I HAD A NEW HAT. THAT'S ALL."

(1938)

"It's my wife—but there's probably some quite simple explanation."

(1949)

Wife: "IF I WERE DEAD WHAT SHOULD YOU DO?"
Husband: "OH, THE SAME AS YOU WOULD IF I WERE DEAD."
Wife: "AH! I ALWAYS SUSPECTED IT."

(1933)

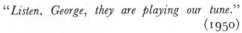

"*Listen, George, they are playing our tune.*"
(1950)

(1952)

"*And that, my lad, is for pinching her from your Commanding Officer.*"
(1948)

". . . and this is my wife's little den."
(1946)

". . . and this is my husband's den."
(1952)

Half-an-hour's rest after meals
(1939)

"You don't have to believe everything you read in the Kinsey Report, you know!"
(1953)

"Of course, we're terribly happy—but then happiness isn't everything."
(1952)

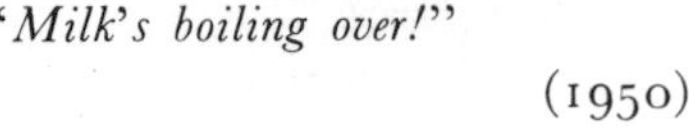

"*Milk's boiling over!*"

(1950)

(1950)

(1948)

"Every night for fifteen years you've walked into this kitchen and said 'Anything I can do?'"

(1950)

"I shan't sleep till he drops the other one."

(1951)

"Good heavens, John! how long were you missing?"

(1954)

"*I think I'm out of my depth this time.*" (1952)

"*Must ring off now, dear, or George'll be screaming for his supper . . .*"

(1952)

(1954)

(1952)

"*I thought you said it had a happy ending!*"

(1946)

GETTING SOMEWHERE

Are women drivers as bad as they are cartooned? Is it really necessary to have the garage door sign-posted DANGER SPOT? When in the Twenties the unpredictable internal-combustion engine was allied to the equally unpredictable woman driver a humour theme was born which has since proved evergreen. The traffic jam is of surprisingly ancient vintage, for Phil May was railing against it in 1903 (see page 121). The early days of railroads led to heavyweight captions, but a century later Emett has done justice to old-time rolling stock (see "For the Duration," page 302 and "Artist's Spot," page 217).

"Of course this means the end of the horse."

(1953)

Railway Official: "YOU'D BETTER NOT SMOKE, SIR!"
Traveller: "THAT'S WHAT MY FRIENDS SAY."
Railway Official: "BUT YOU MUSTN'T SMOKE, SIR!"
Traveller: "SO MY DOCTOR TELLS ME."
Railway Official (indignantly): "BUT YOU SHAN'T SMOKE, SIR!"
Traveller: "AH! JUST WHAT MY WIFE SAYS."

(1853)

ZOOLOGY

Railway Porter (to Old Lady travelling with a Menagerie of Pets): "STATION MASTER SAY, MUM, AS CATS IS 'DOGS,' AND RABBITS IS 'DOGS,' AND SO'S PARROTS; BUT THIS 'ERE 'TORTIS' IS A INSECT, SO THERE AIN'T NO CHARGE FOR IT!"

(1869)

Customer: "LAMP NOT INCLUDED I THE PRICE? WHY, THE LAMP FORM PART OF THE MACHINE IN TH PICTURE!"
Bicycle-Maker: "YES, SIR, BUT A LAD IS ALSO INCLUDED IN THE PICTUR AND WE DON'T GIVE ONE WIT THE MACHINE."

(188

(1905)

"SIT TIGHT, AUNTIE! THERE'S ANOTHER SHARP TURN COMING!"

(1908)

THE LINE OF BEAUTY

Athletic: "DON'T YOU BICYCLE?"

Esthetic: "ER—NO. IT DEVELOPS THE CALVES OF THE LEGS SO! MAKES 'EM STICK OUT, YOU KNOW! SO COARSE! POSITIVE DEFORMITY!"

(1879)

NOT TO BE CAUGHT

Motorist (whose motor has thrown elderly villager into horse-pond): "COME ALONG, MY MAN, I'LL TAKE YOU HOME TO GET DRY."

Elderly Villager: "NO, YER DON'T! I'VE GOT YER NUMBER, AND 'ERE I STAYS TILL A HINDEPENDENT WITNESS COMES ALONG!"

(1906)

Friend: "GOING ABOUT THIRTY, ARE WE? BUT DON'T YOU RUN SOME RISK OF BEING PULLED UP FOR EXCEEDING THE LEGAL PACE?"

Owner: "NOT IN A SOBER, RESPECTABLE-LOOKING CAR LIKE THIS. OF COURSE, IF YOU GO ABOUT IN A BLATANT, BRASS-BOUND, SCARLET-PADDED, SNORTING, FOREIGN AFFAIR LIKE THAT, YOU ARE BOUND TO BE DROPPED ON, NO MATTER HOW SLOW YOU GO!"

(1903)

PROBABLE SCENE IN THE PROXIMITY OF POLICE TRAP, NOW THAT THE PRACTICE OF WARNING MOTORISTS HAS BEEN DECLARED LEGAL.

(1906)

Old Lady (*to Conductor—her first drive on an electric tram*): "WOULD IT BE DANGEROUS, CONDUCTOR, IF I WAS TO PUT MY FOOT ON THE RAIL?"

Conductor: "NO, MUM, NOT UNLESS YOU WAS TO PUT THE OTHER ONE ON THE OVERHEAD WIRE!"

(1908)

Salesman: "AND WHAT KIND OF HORN WOULD YOU LIKE, SIR? DO YOU CARE FOR A GOOD LOUD BLAST?"

Haughty Customer: "NO; I WANT SOMETHING THAT JUST SNEERS."

(1925)

"*I'll take that one.*"
(1952)

LONDON IMPROVEMENTS. AN "OPEN SPACE." (1888)

PRIZE PUZZLE. TO FIND HER WAY ACROSS.

"BUT, OFFICER, THE INSTRUCTION BOOK SAYS QUITE DEFINITELY THAT GREASING SHOULD BE CARRIED OUT EVERY TWO-HUNDRED-AND-FIFTY MILES."

(1938)

(1952)

A QUIET VILLAGE

(1903)

"IT HAS BEEN THE FASTEST ONE OF ITS TYPE IN THE WORLD FOR ALMOST A WEEK NOW."

(1938)

"Beg pardon, but which platform did you say for Derby?"

(1942)

". . . BUT I CAN'T BE IN TWO PLACES AT ONCE, CAN I?"

(1938)

THE BRITISH CHARACTER

LOVE OF TRAVELLING ALONE

(1937)

(1954)

(1951)

"There's the first lie—the booklet said it would cruise happily at sixty all day."

(1954)

"YES, DEAR, I'M BOILING SOME WATER FOR THE RADIATOR—AND I'M HEATING UP A TIN OF PETROL FOR YOU TOO."

(1937)

"DOES YOUR WIFE DRIVE?"
"NO. IT WAS IN THIS CONDITION WHEN I BOUGHT IT."
(1934)

"No, no, Mrs. Williams . . .

"Why it's easy!" (1953)

I'm afraid you'll have to go back . . .

and do it again . . ."

(1951)

(1951)

(1951)

"Gad, sir, vertical take-off! Revolutionary!"

(1954)

(1954)

SATURDAY OFF

(1954)

The Briton's ability to laugh at himself is given full rein in the field of sport. Had he not this ability, most of the pastimes he has chosen for himself would be impossible. Cricket, for instance, is the national Summer game demanding long stretches of fine, warm weather and an acreage of the smoothest turf. Yet, though it is borne in on him year after year that these necessities are not present in quantity in these islands, he carries on.

The Rugger men persist in chasing an oval ball even though the pig's bladder need no longer be used and science can produce a sufficiency of spherical ones. And golf . . . here he has pitted his poor unco-ordinated body against the full forces of nature using the meagrest of weapons. This has led to gloom, fanaticism, divorce but, perversely an ever growing queue at the first tee. Golf could not escape having a full section to itself in this book—see pp. 179-187.

Mrs. Miniver. "HOW EXHAUSTED THEY LOOK, POOR FELLOWS! FANCY DOING THAT SORT OF THING FOR MERE PLEASURE!"

Little Timpkins (*his bosom swelling with national pride*). "AH, BUT IT'S ALL THROUGH DOING THAT SORT OF THING FOR MERE PLEASURE, MIND YOU, THAT WE ENGLISH ARE—WHAT WE ARE!"

[*Bully for little Timpkins!*

(1881)

THE BRITISH CHARACTER

FONDNESS FOR CRICKET (1937)

(1954)

Phil May

Amateur Bowler (to Umpire). "HERE, I SAY! I CAN'T SEE THE WICKET. HOW CAN I BOWL HIM?"

Umpire. "FIRE AWAY! IF YOU 'IT 'IM IN FRONT, IT'S 'LEG BEFORE.' IF YOU 'IT 'IM BEHIND, IT'S A 'WIDE'!" (1901)

He (*as the hope of the team goes in*). "AH! NOW WE HAVE A CHANCE IF HE CAN ONLY GET SOMEONE TO STAY WITH HIM."
She. "IS HE AS DISAGREEABLE AS ALL THAT?" (1912)

"'OW WAS YER OUT, JERRY?"
"CAUGHT AND BOWLED, REUB."
"AH! THEN THEY 'AD YER BOTH WAYS, EH?"
(1912)

A VIOLINIST HAS OCCASION TO ADJUST HIS BATTING-GLOVES. (1921)

Sportsman (*on left*). "IT HARDLY SEEMS RIGHT TO BE GOING TO SEE A CRICKET MATCH WHILE THE REST OF THE WORLD GOES TO WORK."

The Same. "GOOD GRACIOUS! DOESN'T ANYBODY WORK THESE DAYS?" (1921)

IT'S ALL IN THE GAME

(1920)

From a cricket report:—"AFTER LUNCHEON, ROBINSON WAS QUITE UNPLAYABLE, NEITHER BATSMAN BEING ABLE TO GET HIM AWAY." (1922)

Lady (*to Outfield*). "SORRY TO BOTHER YOU, BUT I COULD SEE SO MUCH BETTER IF YOU SAT DOWN." (1921)

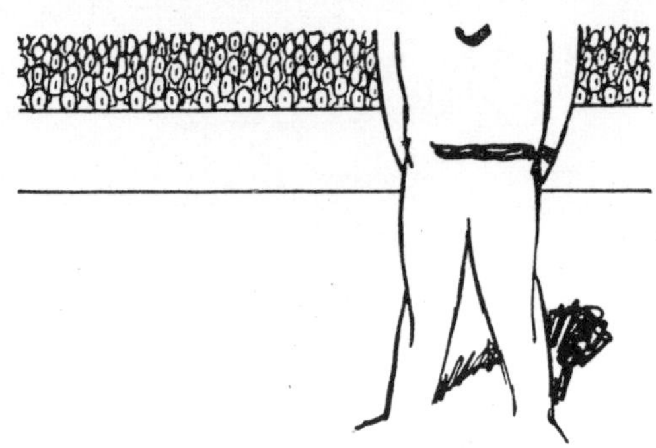

"Would you mind taking middle-and-leg? I'm on TV as well as you, you know."

(1954)

"Then, just as the batsman takes a hefty smack at the ball, you get up and fly straight out over the stand: that NEVER *fails to deceive the customers."*

(1940)

"Hammond says you've had your innings, so why don't you stay and do your share of the fielding like a sportsman?" (1939)

(1956)

Second (whose man's opponent has remained in a crouching position for some time). "SET ABAHT 'IM, CHARLEY. I THINK THE SPRING'S BROKE." (1930)

"You had him worried that round. He thought he'd killed you." (1948)

IT WAS UNFORTUNATE THAT BROWN HAD NOT FINISHED HIS MASTERPIECE, "THE SURRENDER OF THE GARRISON," BY THE TIME THE WAR CAME TO AN END.

HOWEVER, IT NEEDED VERY LITTLE ALTERATION TO MAKE IT SALEABLE.

(1920)

"Is there a doctor on the ground?"

(1956)

(1954)

"And if I see anyone putting less than one hundred per cent into the tackle, I shall know where to find my Ophelia for the Drama Festival."

(1953)

"Staff usually get an early lead, but they tire after the interval."

(1953)

"What does it say about how to serve?"

(1946)

(1952

CLASSICS AND CLICHÉS

No prizes are offered for deciding which are the classics and which are the clichés in this section. A rough division would be that the classics have carried their origin with them wherever they have been quoted, whereas the clichés have long since ceased to be associated with PUNCH and have turned up decade after decade in after-dinner speeches, club conversation, variety and over the air brazenly claiming to be original.

"WHERE ARE YOU OFF TO?"
"TO THE DOCTOR. I DON'T LIKE THE LOOK OF MY WIFE."
"I'LL COME WITH YOU. I HATE THE SIGHT OF MINE."

(1931)

TRUE HUMILITY

Right Reverend Host: "I'M AFRAID YOU'VE GOT A BAD EGG, MR. JONES!"
The Curate: "OH NO, MY LORD, I ASSURE YOU! PARTS OF IT ARE EXCELLENT!"

(1895)

Elder of Fourteen: "WHERE'S BABY, MADGE?"
Madge: "IN THE OTHER ROOM, I THINK, EMILY."
Elder of Fourteen: "GO DIRECTLY, AND SEE WHAT SHE'S DOING, AND TELL HER SHE MUSTN'T."

(1872)

Wife of Two Years' Standing: "OH YES! I'M SURE HE'S NOT SO FOND OF ME AS AT FIRST. HE'S AWAY SO MUCH, NEGLECTS ME DREADFULLY, AND HE'S SO CROSS WHEN HE COMES HOME. WHAT SHALL I DO?"
Widow: "FEED THE BRUTE!"

(1885)

"HULLOA, CHARLIE! WHAT'S THE MATTER? TRAINING FOR A RACE?"
"NO, TOM. RACING FOR A TRAIN!"

(1878)

Sarcastic Peeler: "GOING TO 'AVE A NEW 'ORSE THEN, CABBY?"
Cabby: "NEW OSS, 'OW D'YE MEAN?"
Sarcastic Peeler: "WHY YOU'VE GOT THE FRAMEWORK TOGETHER ALREADY!"

(1861)

Doctor: "NOW, WHAT DID YOUR FATHER AND MOTHER DIE OF?"
Applicant: "WELL, SIR, I CAN'T SAY AS I DO 'XACTLY REMEMBER; BUT 'TWARN'T NOTHING SERIOUS!"

(1896)

A DISCREET (!) FRIEND HAVING PRESENTED MASTER TOM WITH A TOOL-BOX AS A NEW YEAR'S GIFT—THE FURNITURE IS PUT INTO THOROUGH REPAIR.

(1859)

Miss Priscilla: "YES; IT'S A BEAUTIFUL VIEW. BUT TOURISTS ARE IN THE HABIT OF BATHING ON THE OPPOSITE SHORE, AND THAT'S RATHER A DRAWBACK."

Fair Visitor: "DEAR ME! BUT AT SUCH A DISTANCE AS THAT—SURELY—"

Miss Priscilla: "AH, BUT WITH A TELESCOPE, YOU KNOW!"

(1892)

Proud Mamma: "DON'T YOU THINK DEAR BABY'S THE IMAGE OF HIS PAPA?"
Dull but Well-meaning Family Friend: "WELL, PERHAPS HE IS—BUT I DARE SAY HE'LL OUTGROW IT IN TIME."

(1882)

f the House (to caller): "I WANTED TO SEE YOU
›S FATHER SAYS YOU MADE YOURSELF."
: "YES, MY LAD, AND I'M PROUD HOF IT."
f House: "B-BUT WHY DID YOU DO IT LIKE
AT?"

(1913)

Estate Agent (to labourer's son): "HERE, MY BOY, WHERE CAN I FIND YOUR FATHER?"
Boy: "IN THE PIGSTY, SIR. YOU'LL KNOW HIM BY 'IS BROWN 'AT!"

(1903)

THRIFT

Peebles Body (to Townsman who was supposed to be in London on a visit): "E-EH, MAC! YE'RE SUNE HAME AGAIN!"

Mac: "E-EH, IT'S JUST A RUINOUS PLACE, THAT! MUN, A HAD NA' BEEN THE-ERRE ABUNE TWO HOOURS WHEN—BANG—WENT SAXPENCE!!!"

(1868)

A NEW WAY WITH BANKERS

Wife: "BY THE WAY, CLIVE, I HAD A LETTER FROM MY BANKER WHILE YOU WERE AWAY. HE SAID I HAD OVERDRAWN MY ACCOUNT."

Husband: "YES, DEAR; AND WHAT DID YOU DO?"

Wife: "I TOLD HIM NOT TO BE SO RUDE AGAIN; AND I SENT HIM A CHECK FOR THE AMOUNT!"

(1898)

Mabel (not in her first youth): "FIRST OF ALL HE HELD MY HAND AND TOLD MY FORTUNE: AND THEN, EVIE, HE GAZED INTO MY FACE EVER SO LONG, AND SAID HE COULD READ MY THOUGHTS! WASN'T THAT CLEVER OF HIM, DEAR?"

Evie: "OH, I SUPPOSE HE READ BETWEEN THE LINES, DARLING."

(1905)

"SUCH A NICE YOUNG MAN TOOK ME OUT TO DINNER LAST NIGHT—SUCH A WELL-MANNERED MAN. D'YOU KNOW, WHEN THE COFFEE COME AND 'E'D POURED IT IN 'IS SAUCER, INSTEAD OF BLOWING ON IT LIKE A COMMON PERSON, 'E FANNED IT WITH 'IS 'AT!"

(1906)

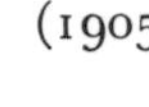

Carrier: "TRY ZIDEWAYS, MRS. JONES, TRY ZIDEWAYS!"
Mrs. Jones: "LAR' BLESS 'EE, JOHN, I AIN'T GOT NO ZIDEWAYS!"

(1900)

Vicar's Wife (sympathizingly): "NOW THAT YOU CAN'T GET ABOUT, AND ARE NOT ABLE TO READ, HOW DO YOU MANAGE TO OCCUPY THE TIME?"
Old Man: "WELL, MUM, SOMETIMES I SITS AND THINKS; AND THEN AGAIN I JUST SITS."

(1906)

Lunatic (*suddenly popping his head over wall*): "WHAT ARE YOU DOING THERE?"
Brown: "FISHING."
Lunatic: "CAUGHT ANYTHING?"
Brown: "NO."
Lunatic: "HOW LONG HAVE YOU BEEN THERE?"
Brown: "SIX HOURS."
Lunatic: "COME INSIDE!"

(1897)

"D'YOU SERVE LOBSTERS?"
"YESSIR, WE SERVE ANYBODY."

(1933)

"SUSAN, JUST LOOK HERE! I CAN WRITE MY NAME IN THE DUST ON THE TOP OF THIS TABLE!"
"LOR, MUM, SO YOU CAN! NOW I NEVER HAD NO EDGERCATION MYSELF!"

(1895)

Brown-Smith (who has been paying for everything): "SUPPOSE YOU PAY THIS TIME AND I'LL FUMBLE."

(1923)

"I WANT TO PAY THE LAST INSTALMENT ON THE BABY'S PRAM."
"THANK YOU, MADAM. THE BABY, I TRUST, IS QUITE WELL?"
"YES, THANKS. SHE'S GETTING MARRIED NEXT WEEK."

(1930)

nining Admiral (to naval candidate): "NOW MENTION THREE GREAT DMIRALS."
lidate: "DRAKE, NELSON AND — I BEG YOUR PARDON, SIR, I DN'T QUITE CATCH YOUR NAME."

(1914)

WOMAN—EVER UNREASONABLE

"HANDS UP! OR I FIRE!!"

(1904)

She: "WHAT DO YOU THINK OF HIS EXECUTION?"
He: "I'M IN FAVOUR OF IT."

(1907)

Nervous Suitor: "I—ER—WISH TO MARRY YOUR DAUGHTER, SIR!"
Parent: "WELL, MY BOY, HADN'T YOU BETTER SEE HER MOTHER FIRST?"
Nervous Suitor: "I HAVE, SIR, AND—ER—ER—I STILL WISH TO MARRY YOUR DAUGHTER."

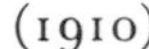

(1910)

Chemist: "PILLS, EH?" (*Emphasizing question.*) "ANTI-BILIOUS?"
Child (*readily*)*:* "NO, SIR; UNCLE IS!"

(1901)

Poor Golfer: "I THINK THE TROUBLE WITH ME IS THAT I STAND TOO NEAR THE BALL BEFORE DRIVE."
Caddie: "MAY BE—AN' YOU OFTEN STAND TOO NEAR IT AFTER YOU DRIVE TOO."

(1924)

Dear Old Soul: "I AM SOLICITING FOR THE NEEDY, MR. JONES. WHAT DO YOU DO WITH YOUR OLD CLOTHES?"
Mr. Jones (*one of the New Poor*)*:* "I BRUSH AND FOLD THEM CAREFULLY, AND THEN PUT THEM ON AGAIN IN THE MORNING."

(1921)

"THEY HAD THE CHEEK TO SAY THERE WASN'T A SINGLE ROOM IN THE WHOLE BLASTED PLACE. WE WERE SIMPLY FURIOUS, SO WE TOLD 'EM WHO WE WERE."
"REALLY, AND WHO WERE YOU?"

(1933)

Wife. "I'VE BOUGHT SUCH A DUCK OF A SALOON-CAR TO-DAY, DEAR. THE SALESMAN SAID WE COULD PAY BY INSTALMENTS—ONLY TWELVE POUNDS A MONTH!"

Husband. "FOR HOW MANY MONTHS?"

Wife. "OH, I FORGOT TO ASK!"

(1928)

Holiday-maker. "I'LL HAVE A COUPLE OF KIDLEYS."

Waitress. "D'YOU MEAN KIDNEYS?"

Holiday-maker. "WELL, DIDL'T I SAY KIDLEYS?"

(1932)

BLESS THEM!

Some tormentor invented children and I approve the opinion of Euripides, who said that they which had no children are happy by being unfortunate.

BOETHIUS A.D. 524

Cute, precocious, tough and burgeoning with private domestic truth on public occasions, the children in PUNCH have been well served by their artists. J. H. Dowd's solid, earthy children are in a class of their own. His "What did I learn?" on p. 160 should really be in the "Classics" section.

"YOU CAN'T MARRY GRETA GARBO UNTIL YOU GROW UP, SO DO STOP BEING A BABY ABOUT IT."

(1938)

(1954)

"WHY DO YOU PUT YOUR DOLLS BY SO CAREFULLY, MAGGIE?"

"I AM KEEPING THEM FOR MY CHILDREN."

"BUT SUPPOSE YOU DON'T HAVE ANY CHILDREN?"

"THEN THEY WILL DO FOR MY GRANDCHILDREN!"

(1871)

Parson: "WHAT'S A MIRACLE?"

Boy: "DUNNO."

Parson: "WELL, IF THE SUN WERE TO SHINE IN THE MIDDLE OF THE NIGHT, WHAT SHOULD YOU SAY IT WAS?"

Boy: "THE MOON."

Parson: "BUT IF YOU WERE TOLD IT WAS THE SUN, WHAT SHOULD YOU SAY IT WAS?"

Boy: "A LIE."

Parson: "I DON'T TELL LIES. SUPPOSE I TOLD YOU IT WAS THE SUN; WHAT WOULD YOU SAY THEN?"

Boy: "THAT YER WASN'T SOBER!"

(1871)

NOT TO BE BEATEN

"MY MAMMA'S GOT THE SHININGEST HAIR IN ALL BAYSWATER."

"MY MAMMA'S GOT THE CURLINGEST HAIR IN ALL LONDON."

"MY MAMMA'S GOT THE LONGEST HAIR IN ALL ENGLAND."

"MY MAMMA'S GOT THE THICKEST HAIR IN ALL THE WHOLE WORLD."

"MY MAMMA CAN SIT ON HER HAIR."

"MY MAMMA CAN TAKE HERS OFF!!!"

(1871)

Mamma: "NOW GO AND SAY GOOD NIGHT TO YOUR GOVERNESS, LIKE A GOOD LITTLE GIRL, AND GIVE HER A KISS."

Little Puss: "I'LL SAY GOOD NIGHT, BUT I WON'T GIVE HER A KISS."

Mamma: "THAT'S NAUGHTY! WHY WON'T YOU GIVE HER A KISS?"

Little Puss: "BECAUSE SHE SLAPS PEOPLE'S FACES WHEN THEY TRY TO KISS HER."

Mamma: "NOW, DON'T TALK NONSENSE; BUT DO AS YOU'RE TOLD."

Little Puss: "WELL, MUMMY, IF YOU DON'T BELIEVE ME,—ASK PAPA!"

(1900)

Governess: "NOW, LINSLEY, YOU MUSTN'T HAVE ANY MORE PLUM PUDDING. IT'LL MAKE YOU ILL!"

Linsley: "NEVER MIND, IT'S WORF IT!"

(1898)

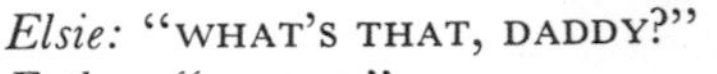

Elsie: "WHAT'S THAT, DADDY?"

Father: "A COW."

Elsie: "WHY?"

(1906)

Mabel (stroking kitten, a new present): "MOTHER, KITTY'S SO HOT! OUGHT SHE TO SIT SO NEAR THE FIRE?" *(Kitten purrs.)* "OH, MOTHER, LISTEN! SHE'S BEGINNING TO BOIL!"

(1900)

Mamma: "YOU MUSTN'T BOWL YOUR HOOP IN THE FRONT ON SUNDAY. YOU MUST GO INTO THE BACK GARDEN."
Tommy: "ISN'T IT SUNDAY IN THE BACK GARDEN, MAMMA?"

(1902)

ENFANT TERRIBLE

Family Doctor: "I HOPE, MY DEAR LADY, THAT YOU ARE ALL THE BETTER FOR YOUR LONG HOLIDAY AND THOROUGH CHANGE OF AIR."
The Patient: "IT HAS DONE ME ALL THE GOOD IN THE WORLD, MY DEAR DOCTOR. I AM A DIFFERENT BEING; IN FACT, QUITE ANOTHER WOMAN!"
Sharp Child: "OH, MAMMA! HOW PLEASED PAPA WILL BE WHEN HE HEARS THIS!"

(1903)

Old Admiral: "WHAT ANIMALS EAT GRASS?" *(Long pause.)*
Old Admiral (helpfully): "WELL, COME, HORSES EAT GRASS, FOR INSTANCE, DON'T THEY?"
Candidate (with great relief): "OH, ANIMALS! I THOUGHT YOU SAID ADMIRALS!"

(1906)

BEGINNING EARLY

Dorothy: "OH, MAMMA DEAR, EVERY DAY WHEN I GO TO SCHOOL, A NAUGHTY LITTLE BOY WILL KISS ME!"

Mamma: "WELL, DARLING, YOU SHOULD RUN AWAY."

Dorothy: "WELL, BUT—SUPPOSE HE DIDN'T RUN AFTER ME!"

(1898)

Small Student of Natural History: "I SAY, MABEL, DO HEDGEHOGS LAY EGGS, OR DO THEY HAVE KITTENS, LIKE RABBITS?"

(1921)

Little Boy: "MOTHER, DID GRAN'PA THRASH DADDY WHEN HE WAS A LITTLE BOY?"

Mother: "YES."

Boy: "AND DID HIS FATHER THRASH HIM WHEN HE WAS A LITTLE BOY?"

Mother: "YES."

Boy: "AND DID HIS FATHER THRASH HIM?"

Mother: "YES."

Boy: "WELL, WHO STARTED THIS THING?"

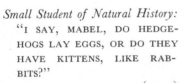

(1913)

Basil: "MOTHER, HOW IS IT THAT SOLDIERS' MUSIC ALWAYS MAKES ME FEEL SO MUCH HAPPIER THAN I REALLY AM?"

(1909)

"WHAT ARE TORIES AND RADICALS, GRANDPAPA?"

"TORIES, MY DEAR, ARE PEOPLE WHO LIKE TO HAVE A QUEEN, AND LORDS, AND BISHOPS, AND MORE OR LESS REMAIN AS THEY ARE—WHILST RADICALS OBJECT TO HAVING A QUEEN AND A HOUSE OF LORDS, AND ARE DISSATISFIED WITH EVERYTHING AND EVERYBODY, JEALOUS OF ALL WHO ARE BETTER OFF THAN THEMSELVES, AND ARE ALWAYS TRYING TO ROB THEM OF THEIR PROPERTY, AND, IN FACT, THEY'RE A PACK OF INFERNAL ROGUES AND SCOUNDRELS!"

"AND WHICH ARE YOU, GRANDPAPA—A TORY OR A RADICAL?"

(1896)

Mother (after relating pathetic story): "NOW, REGGIE, WOULDN'T YOU LIKE TO GIVE YOUR BUNNY TO THAT POOR LITTLE BOY YOU SAW TODAY WHO HASN'T ANY FATHER?"

Reggie (clutching rabbit): "COULDN'T WE GIVE HIM FATHER INSTEAD?"

(1913)

Boy: "PLEASE, TEACHER, WHAT DID I LEARN TODAY?"
Teacher: "THAT'S A PECULIAR QUESTION."
Boy: "WELL, THEY'LL ASK ME WHEN I GET HOME."
(1929)

Molly (*at the jam-cupboard*): "WON'T ANY OF THE KEYS FIT, BOBBY?"
Bobby: "NO."
Molly: "THEN LET'S WAIT TILL MUMMY COMES BACK AND GET HER TO GIVE US SOMETHING FOR BEING GOOD."
(1928)

Pamela: "HOW'S YOUR WIFE, PETER?"
Peter: "SHE DIED LAST TUESDAY."
Pamela: "ARE YOU SORRY?"
Peter: "SORRY? OF COURSE I'M SORRY. I LIKED THE WOMAN."
(1927)

Mother: "WHAT ARE YOU DOING?"
Child: "GARDENING, MUMMY."
Mother: "BUT THAT ISN'T GARDENING."
Child: "WELL, THAT'S HOW DADDY DOES IT."

(1925)

Mother: "DORIS, DEAR, WHY DO YOU ALWAYS ASK ME TO READ THIS SAD, SAD POEM?"
Doris: "I LIKE SAD POEMS; THEY MAKE MY NOSE ITCH."

(1928)

A DAY IN THE COUNTRY

Little Tommy (who has never been out of Whitechapel before): "OH! OH! OH!
Kind Lady: "WHATS THE MATTER, TOMMY?"
Little Tommy: "WHY, WHAT A BIG SKY THEY'VE GOT 'ERE, MISS!"

(1887)

Hospital Patient (one of large family in poor district, given a glass of milk): "HOW FAR DOWN CAN I DRINK?"

(1932)

"THIS PROVES WHAT I'VE ALWAYS MAINTAINED; PARENTS ARE PRECISELY THE PEOPLE WHO OUGHT NOT TO HAVE CHILDREN."

(1933)

Schoolmaster: "AND—ER—WHAT PROFESSION DOES THE YOUNG MAN PROPOSE TO FOLLOW?"
Parent: "WELL, HE SAYS HE WANTS TO BE A CHEMIST."
Schoolmaster: "A CHEMIST, EH? ANALYTICAL—DISPENSING—"
The Young Man (firmly): "CASH."

(1932)

Father: "WELL, WOT DID THEY LEARN YER AT SUNDAY SCHOOL?"
Betty: "THAT I'M A CHILD OF SATAN."

(1933)

"Does it tick?"

(1946)

"WHAT HAVE YOU GOT IN THAT BAG, TEACHER?"
"MY WAGES, JOHNNIE."
"WAGES! WHY, WHERE DO YOU WORK, MISS?"

(1937)

"IS THAT A NICE BOOK, DARLING?"
"IT'S LOVELY, MUMMY, BUT THE ENDING'S SAD."
"WHAT HAPPENS?"
"OH, SHE DIES, AND HE HAS TO GO BACK TO HIS WIFE."

(1932)

"Mummy, it's leaking."

(1946)

"I know what they're thinking. They're thinking what a shabby old saucepan to let a boy get his head stuck into."

(1951)

"Don't interfere, dear. He's got to learn by his mistakes."

(1948)

"Isn't there anything we mustn't do?"

(1952)

(194

(1949)

"*See! It keeps missing.*"
(1947)

"OF COURSE WE MUST FACE FACTS. IT'S GOING TO MEAN WAITING."
(1940)

(1947)

(1950)

". . . and what's more he'll remain in the cellar until he's in a more repentant frame of mind."

(1950)

"Look what I found on top of the wardrobe."

(1954)

(1952)

"A supersonic turbo-jet atomic bomber, please, and a doll that rolls its eyes and says 'Mama.'"

(1952)

(1946)

UNRECORDED HISTORY

History is something that never happened, written by a man who wasn't there.

ANON

"NO BATHING TODAY!"

(1894)

AGRICOLA LECTURING THE ANCIENT BRITONS ON THE ADVANTAGES OF ROMAN CIVILIZATION

(1912)

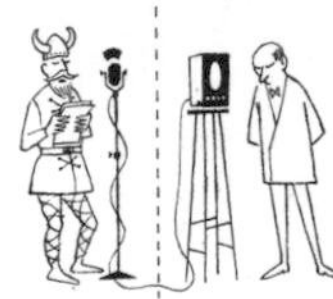

SCENE ON THE UPPER DECK OF THE ARK. THE GIRAFFE BEGINS TO FEEL THE MOTION.

(1950)

QUEEN ELIZABETH JUST RUNS THROUGH A LITTLE THING OF HER OWN COMPOSITION TO WILLIAM SHAKESPEARE.

(1896)

THE CONSTITUTIONAL INABILITY OF GEORGE WASHINGTON TO TELL A LIE WAS PROVERBIAL, AND THE HOPE OF SOME OF HIS SUPPORTERS THAT LATE IN LIFE THIS PHYSICAL DEFECT MIGHT BE OVERCOME, WAS DOOMED TO DISAPPOINTMENT. A DIPLOMATIC HYPERBOLE WAS THE BEST HE COULD EVER DO IN SPITE OF MOST PRAISEWORTHY EFFORTS.

(1896)

THE KING'S REMEMBRANCER TACTFULLY REMINDS HENRY VIII THAT HIS MAJESTY HAS ALREADY BEEN MARRIED FIVE TIMES.

(1912)

Ethelred the Unready causes an Obstruction at a Tube Booking Office.

Caxton is overcome by one of the familiar Objects of our Streets.

Richard III, having offered his Kingdom for a Horse, can get nothing but a Taxi.

Chaucer unfortunately misses the Canterbury Excursion Train.

(1911)

"This is what comes of marrying a career woman."

(1950)

"It looks as if there's been a breakdown in our negotiations with the management."

(1951)

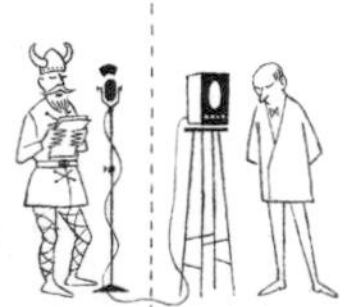

"Very well then, hands up all those who propose to become birds."

(1951)

"You're fired!"

(1952)

"Laugh, please."

(1953)

"Oh Lord! Here he goes again."

(1953)

"Seems they had quite a party."

(1950)

"Personally, I can't see that there'll ever be the slightest demand for this stuff in the old country." (1947)

"Merely by twisted elastic!" (1952)

"Ah, well, 'Many a true word spoken in jest'." (1952)

SCRATCH

FOR THE COURSE

I must go down to the links again,
  To the rolling links and the sand,
And all I ask is a new ball
  And a club to fit my hand;
And the ball's click and the club's swing
  And a boy to caddy for me,
And the gray look on the foe's face
  When the lad says "Dormy!"

I must go down to the links again,
  For the call of the bunker wide
Is a wild call and a clear call
  That may not be denied;
And all I ask is a windless day,
  With the white balls rolling,
And the "rough" short and the greens true,
  And my long putts holing.

MARCUS DODS

(*With apologies to John Masefield's "Sea Fever"*)

(1920)

THE WOMAN-HATER

Mr. Meenister MacGlucky (of the Free Kirk, after having given way more than usual to an expression "a wee thing strong"—despairingly): "OH! AYE! AH, W-E-EL! I'LL HAE TA GIE 'T UP!"

Mr. Elder MacNab: "WH-AT, MAN, GIE UP GOWF?"

Mr. Meenister MacGlucky: "NAE, NAE! GIE UP THE MEENISTRY!"

(1895)

A beautiful stroke missed! A favourite club broken! No words to bring relief!

American Friend (in the background, after a long pause): "WE'AL, BROWN, I GUESS THAT'S THE MOST PROFANE SILENCE I'VE EVER LISTENED TO!"

(1903)

A LAST RESORT

Miss Armstrong (who has foozled the ball six times with various clubs): "AND WHICH OF THE STICKS I TO USE NOW?"

Weary Caddie: "GIE IT A BIT KNOCK WI' THE BAG!"

(19

THE ENGLISH WIFE

THE AMERICAN HUSBAND

(1905)

THE BULLDOG BREED

Sportsman (whose opponent has just achieved the hole in one): "THIS FOR A HALF!"

(1920)

Bobby (following mother and father round links at a respectful distance): "I WONDER WHO'S WINNING?"

Peggy: "I THINK FATHER MUST BE. I HEARD HIM OFFER TO CARRY MOTHER'S CLUBS A FEW MINUTES AGO."

(1924)

First Golfer: "I SAY, OLD MAN, THAT'S ROTTEN GOLF."
Second Golfer: "YES; BUT IT'S THUNDERING FINE CROQUET. WHAT?"

(1908)

Bride (determined to share her husband's troubles): "DEAREST, GO ON TELLING ME ABOUT THE WORM-CASTS ON THE SEVENTEENTH."

(1908)

Caddie (in charge of beginner): "LUMMY, MISS, YOU BEEN AND DONE IT IN ONE!"

Beginner: "I'M TERRIBLY SORRY. WHAT <u>SHOULD</u> I HAVE DONE?"

(1928)

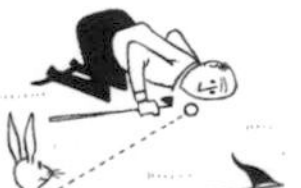

Small Boy (walking round with his father): "DADDY, HERE'S A BALL FOR YOU."

Father: "WHERE DID YOU GET THAT FROM?"

Small Boy: "IT'S A LOST BALL, DADDY."

Father: "ARE YOU SURE IT'S A LOST BALL?"

Small Boy: "YES, DADDY; THEY'RE STILL LOOKING FOR IT."

(1921)

First Player: "MY WIFE THREATENS TO LEAVE ME IF I DON'T CHUCK GOLF."

Second Player: "THAT SOUNDS SERIOUS."

First Player: "IT <u>IS</u> SERIOUS. I SHALL MISS HER."

(1931)

Small Girl (*as golfer pauses for breath*): "HE'S STOPPED BEATING IT, MUMMY. I THINK IT MUST BE DEAD."

(1930)

efeated Player in Club Final: "ISN'T IT DREADFUL, BURGESS? FANCY BEING BEATEN 8 AND 7! I SHALL NEVER BE ABLE TO LIFT UP MY HEAD AGAIN."
urgess: "WELL, YOU DONE IT IN THE MATCH ALL RIGHT."

(1929)

Beginner (after repeated failures): "FUNNY GAME, GOLF."
Caddie: "'TAIN'T MEANT TO BE."

(1931)

NATURE'S WAY

HIS MASTER'S DAUGHTER—

HAS NONE OF HIS MASTER'S REVERENCE FOR THEORY.

ALSO, UNLIKE HIS MASTER'S—

HER PUTTS GO IN!

(1928)

NDUCED BY THE CLUB BORE

(1924)

(1949)

(1949)

(195

(1955)

"HALLO! WHAT'S THE IDEA OF THE WATCH?"
"'TAIN'T A WATCH, SIR; IT'S A COMPASS."

(1936)

ngle Thruster: "IN THE ORDINARY WAY OF COURSE I SHOULDN'T THINK OF ASKING YOU TO LET ME COME THROUGH; BUT I'VE JUST HEARD MY WIFE HAS MET WITH A SERIOUS ACCIDENT."

(1931)

Hopeless Golfer: "WHAT COULDN'T I DO TO A NICE BIG BOTTLE OF BEER?"
Caddie (scornfully): "HIT IT WITH A CLUB."

(1931)

BEGORRAH!

The "Bull" or inadvertent contradiction is a form of humour credited to the loquacious Irish, but many "Bulls" have been perpetrated that never had benefit of shamrock or shillelagh.

PRIMA FACIE

Magistrate: "THE EVIDENCE SHOWS THAT YOU THREW A STONE AT THIS MAN."

Mrs. O'Hooligan: "FAITH, THEN, THE LOOKS O' THE BASTE SHOWS BETTER 'N THAT, YER HONOR. THEY SHOWS I 'IT 'IM!"

(1906)

LATEST RAILWAY MARVEL

Gent: "I SAY, PORTER, WHEN DOES THE NEXT TRAIN START?"

Irish Porter: "THE NEXT TRAIN! SURE, THE NIXT TRAIN HAS GONE TIN MINUTES AGO."

(1871)

THE VERDICT

First Irishman (waiting in the Corridor—to his Friend, rushing in from the Court): "WHAT'S TIM GOT?"

Second Irishman (in a breathless whisper): "FOR LOIFE!"

First Irishman: "FOR LOIFE!" (With emotion.) "OCH, SHURE, HE WON'T LIVE HALF THE THOIME!!"

(1884)

Mick: "I HEAR 'TIS THE WAY THEY'RE AFTHER SENDIN' MESSAGES NOW WIDOUT WIRES OR POLES. FAITH, 'TIS WONDHERFUL TIMES WE'RE LIVIN' IN, DENNIS."

Dennis: "THRUE FOR YOU, MICK. SHURE THE WAY THINGS IS GOIN', WAN OF THESE DAYS WE'LL BE ABLE TO THRAVEL WIDOUT LAVIN' HOME AT ALL, AT ALL."

(1910)

Mrs. O'Brady: "SHURE I WANT TO BANK TWINTY POUNDS. CAN I DRAW IT OUT QUICK IF I WANT IT?"

Postmaster: "INDADE, MRS. O'BRADY, YOU CAN DRAW IT OUT TOMORROW IF YOU GIVE ME A WAKE'S NOTICE!"

(1901)

Judge (to Witness): "REPEAT THE PRISONER'S STATEMENT TO YOU, EXACTLY IN HIS OWN WORDS. NOW, WHAT DID HE SAY?"

Witness: "MY LORD, HE SAID HE STOLE THE PIG—"

Judge: "IMPOSSIBLE! HE COULDN'T HAVE USED THE THIRD PERSON."

Witness: "MY LORD, THERE WAS NO THIRD PERSON!"

Judge: "NONSENSE! I SUPPOSE YOU MEAN THAT HE SAID, 'I STOLE THE PIG!' "

Witness (shocked): "OH, MY LORD! HE NEVER MENTIONED YOUR LORDSHIP'S NAME!"

(*Dismissed ignominiously.*)

(1884)

Prisoner: "SORR, I OBJECT TO MR. CLANCY SERVIN' ON THE JURY."
Mr. Clancy: "BEDAD, AN' FOR WHY, MICHAEL? I'M FOR YEZ."

(1920)

Policeman: "WOT ARE YER STANDING 'ERE FOR?"
Loafer: "NUFFINK."
Policeman: "WELL, JUST MOVE ON. IF EVERYBODY WAS TO STAND IN ONE PLACE 'OW WOULD THE REST GET PAST?"

(1925)

A CONTINTED MIND
Tirence (Bricklayer's Labourer, acclimatized, to Paddy [just] from Cork): "SELL YER PIG AN' FOURNICHURE AN' COME OVER WID BIDDY TO THIS BLISSED COUNTRY. I GET TREE AN' T'RIPENCE A DAY FOR CARR'IN' BRICKS UP A LADDER, AN', BE JABERS, THERE'S A POOR DIVIL UP AT THE TOP DOIN' ALL THE WORK FOR ME!!"

(1873)

The Colonel (stopping at Irish Inn): "LOOK HERE! WHAT'S THE MEANING OF THIS?"
Boots: "BEDAD! AN' I'VE GOT JUST SUCH ANOTHER QUARE PAIR DOWN BELOW!"

(1903)

Cobbler (to customer who wants his boots repaired at once): "CAN'T DO 'EM TILL WEDNESDAY."
Customer: "BUT YOU ANNOUNCE 'REPAIRS WHILE YOU WAIT.'"
Cobbler: "AY—AND YOU'LL HAVE TO WAIT TILL WEDNESDAY."

(1925)

"HI! BILL! DON'T COME DOWN THIS LADDER. I'VE TOOK IT AWAY!

(1917)

"THIS IS A BUILT-UP AREA, MADAM, AND YOU 'VE BEEN GOIN' MORE THAN THIRTY MILES AN HOUR."
"DON'T BE SILLY. I HAVEN'T BEEN OUT AN HOUR YET."

(1935)

THOSE WHO SERVE . . .
AND SOMETIMES ANSWER BACK

"That will be all for this evening, Barker."
(1947)

WHERE HAVE YOU BEEN, JANE?"
'VE BEEN TO A MEETING OF THE GIRLS' FRIEND-LY SOCIETY, MA'AM."
VELL, AND WHAT DID THE LADY SAY TO YOU?"
LEASE, MA'AM, SHE SAID I WASN'T TO GIVE YOU WARNING, AS I MEANT TO. SHE SAID I WAS TO LOOK UPON YOU AS MY THORN——AND BEAR IT!"

(1886)

A SECRET OF THE SEA

Passenger: "LOOK HERE, STEWARD, IF THIS IS COFFEE, I WANT TEA; BUT IF THIS IS TEA, THEN I WISH FOR COFFEE."

(1902)

t Party: "NOW THEN, WAITER, WHAT HAVE OU GOT?"
iter: "CALVES' BRAINS, DEVILED KIDNEYS, RIED LIVER—"
t Party: "HERE! BOTHER YOUR COMPLAINTS! IVE ME THE MENOO."

(1901)

"DON'T YOU THINK, JAMES, THAT THESE LONELY DINNERS AT THE CLUB DRIVE A NUMBER OF MEN TO MATRIMONY?"
"MAY BE, SIR; BUT NOT SO MANY AS MATRIMONY DRIVES TO THE CLUB."

(1898)

The Waiter (who is on a week's notice): "DID YOU HAVE TOMATO OR PEA SOUP, SIR?"
The Customer: "HEAVEN KNOWS! IT TASTED MORE LIKE SOAP."
The Waiter: "AH, THAT WOULD BE TOMATO, SIR. THE PEA SOUP TASTES LIKE PARAFFIN."

(1922)

Customer: "I'LL HAVE THAT ECLAIR."
Waiter: "THAT, MADAM, IS MY THUMB."

(1922)

Country Hotel Waiter: "YOU WISHED YOUR COFFEE WITHOUT CREAM, SIR. I'M SORRY, WE HAVE NO CREAM. WILL YOU HAVE IT WITHOUT MILK?"

(1928)

SEASONED

Lady Tourist: "ARE THE SHEETS WELL AIRED?"
Irish Chambermaid: "TROTH, AND THEY ARE, MA'AM; FOR THE SEASON IS THREE MONTHS BEGUN, AND THEY'VE BEEN WELL USED SINCE!"

(1879)

Wife: "I WISH YOU'D SPEAK TO THE BUTLER."
Insignificant Husband: "WHY SHOULD I? HE NEVER SPEAKS TO ME."

(1930)

Lady (engaging servant for country cottage): "OF COURSE THERE ARE NO LAMPS TO DO. YOU SEE, I HAVE THE ELECTRIC LIGHT."
Mother: "WELL, MUM, SHE'S A BRIGHT GIRL, AND SHE'LL SOON MASTER THE ELECTRIC LIGHT."

(1929)

"WHAT DO YOU CALL THIS PLACE?"
"YE OLDE TUDOR CHOPPE HOUSE."
"WELL, I CAN'T CUT YE OLDE TUDOR CHOPPE."
(1933)

Habitué (introducing his wife to favourite hotel): "HERE, WAITER, WHERE'S MY HONEY?"
Waiter: "I'M SORRY, SIR, BUT SHE DOESN'T WORK HERE NOW."
(1922)

"I KNOW, SIR, BUT YOU DIDN'T HAVE THE CELE
YOU HAD THE DAFFODILS."
(19

"*And if you want anything, just ring.*"
(1946)

"*Sorry we are so full at the Rectory, but just ring if you want anything.*"
(1948)

Gloomy Diner: "WHICH OF YOUR BEASTLY WINES WILL INDUCE OBLIVION?"
(1930)

"*And now What shall we do with the Drunken Sailor?' for Miss Ellen Bates, The Moorings, Mudthorpe-on-Sea.*"
(1946)

THE ARTISTS' CORNER

All the artists represented in this section have drawings in other parts of the book, but by putting a group of each artist's drawings together you can get a better idea of his style of humour.

EASTER MONDAY

'Arry: "DO YOU PASS ANY PUBS ON THE WAY TO BROADSTAIRS, CABBY?"
Cabby: "YES. LOTS."
'Arry: "WELL, DON'T!"

(1898)

Q. E. D.

"WHAT'S UP WI' SAL?" "AIN'T YER ERD? SHE'S MARRIED AGIN!"

(1894)

FOGGY WEATHER

"HAS MR. SMITH BEEN HERE?"
"YES; HE WAS HERE ABOUT AN HOUR AGO."
"WAS I WITH HIM?"

(1894)

"ARE YOU COMIN' 'OME?"
"I'LL DO ELLYTHIK YOU LIKE IN REASON, M'RIA—(*hic*)— BUT I WON'T COME 'OME."

(1895)

THE MAN WHO PAID OFF HIS OVERDRAFT
(1930)

A MATTER OF POLICY

HOW VERY PAINFUL IT IS TO BE PRESENT WHEN ONE'S HOST AND HOSTESS BECOME INVOLVED IN A SERIOUS ALTERCATION.

WHAT IS THE BEST THING TO DO? AFFECT TO NOTICE NOTHING?

OR BECOME ABSORBED IN THE SURROUNDING OBJECTS OF ART?

PERHAPS DROPPING SOMETHING TO CREATE A DIVERSION?

OR SHOULD ONE SWITCH ON THEIR WIRELESS?

OR TREAT IT AS A JOKE AND LAUGH HEARTILY?

OR SHOULD ONE TAKE SIDES AND TRY TO SETTLE THE DISPUTE FINALLY?

(1931)

ANYTHING IN THE PAPER, DARLING?

ABSOLUTELY NOTHING

THOMAS DERRICK

NEWS
(1938)

THREE-ACT COMEDY
(1935)

Oldest Inhabitant (*to District Visitor*): "I BE NINETY-FOUR AND I 'AVEN'T GOT AN ENEMY IN THE WORLD."
District Visitor: "THAT IS A BEAUTIFUL THOUGHT."
Oldest Inhabitant: "YES, MISS. THANK GOD THEY BE ALL OF 'EM DEAD LONG AGO!"

(1931)

"AS I ALWAYS SEZ, MRS. GREEN, ONE 'ARF THE WORLD DON'T KNOW WOT THE OTHER 'ARF'S DOIN'."
"WELL, THAT AIN'T YOUR FAULT, DEARIE, IS IT, NOW?"

(1933)

Exasperated Bos'n: "IF YER BRAINS WAS DYNAMITE THEY WOULDN'T BLOW YER BLINKIN' 'AT OFF!"

(1923)

HOW TO GET ON IN THE NAVY

Sailor: "BUT LOOK 'ERE, RUFUS. SUPPOSIN' I DID BUY IT, WHAT AM I GOING TO DO WITH A FLAMIN' CALICO CAMEL?"

Rug Merchant: "YOU PUTTA DA MAT IN DA CAPITAN'S CABIN, AN' DA CAPITAN SO PLEASED THAT HE GIVVA YOU DA PROMOTION."

(1922)

Sailor (to passenger caught on hook of crane): "WHILST YOU'RE ABOUT IT, SIR, BEST LET 'EM SWING YOU STRAIGHT ON BOARD. I'LL BRING YOUR 'AT."

(1930)

THE ANNUAL DINNER OF THE OMAR KHAYYAM SOCIETY

(1925)

"BALANCING THE BOOKS" AT THE ANNUAL DINNER OF THE SOCIETY OF CHARTERED ACCOUNTANTS

(1931)

AT THE END OF AN EXCEPTIONALLY SMOOTH PASSAGE THE CAPTAIN DECORATES THE ONLY PASSENGER WHO HAS REFRAINED FROM USING THE EXPRESSION "MILL POND."

(1932)

A MASS MEETING OF ABSENT-MINDED PROFESSORS HAS BEEN CALLED TO PROTEST AGAINST JOKES ABOUT THEM IN THE COMIC PAPERS.

(1935)

THE BRITISH CHARACTER

LOVE OF KEEPING CALM.

(1937)

THE BRITISH CHARACTER

ADAPTABILITY TO FOREIGN CONDITIONS.

(1934)

THE BRITISH CHARACTER

LOVE OF NEVER THROWING ANYTHING AWAY.

(1937)

THE BRITISH CHARACTER

A TENDENCY TO THINK THINGS NOT SO GOOD AS THEY USED TO BE.

(1937)

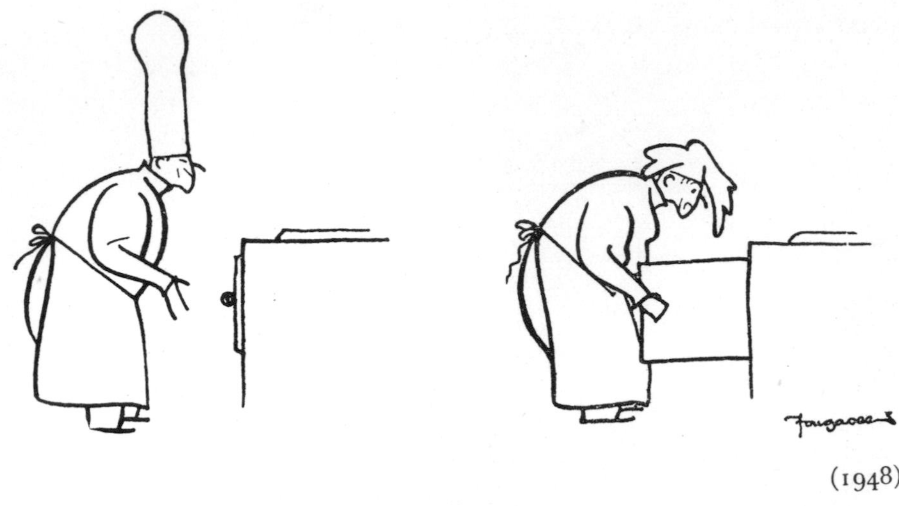

(1948)

THE SOUFFLÉ

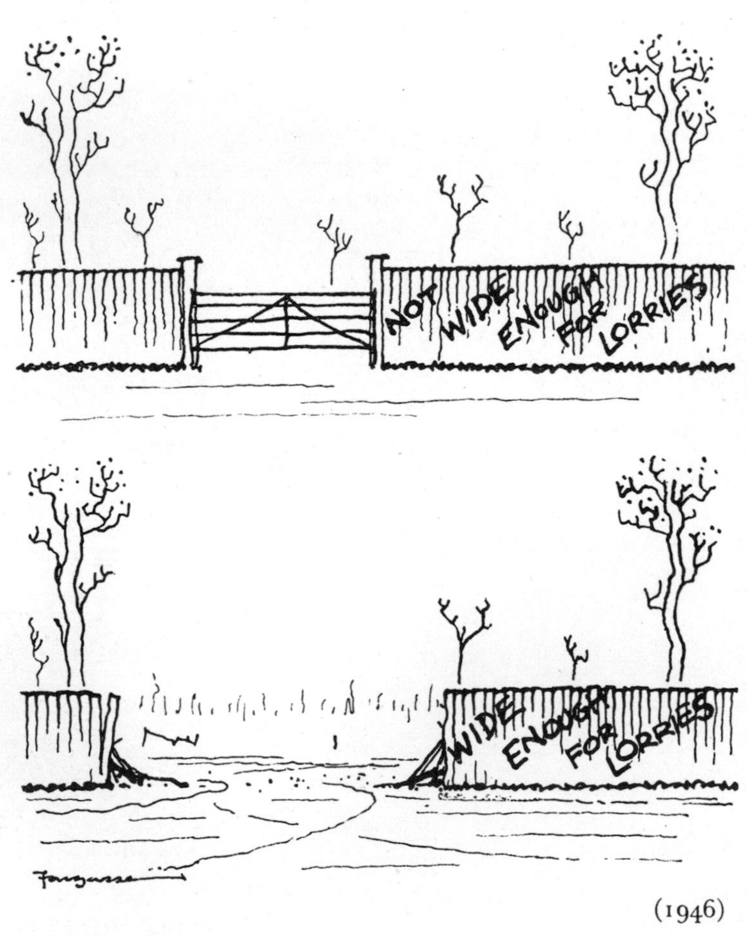

(1946)

"YOU REMEMBER, MARTHA

MY TELLING YOU—

HOW I'D HAD A DREAM—

THAT I HAD TO GIVE—

A VERY IMPORTANT LECTURE—

AND HOW WHEN I GOT THERE—

I COULDN'T REMEMBER—

WHAT I HAD TO LECTURE ABOUT—

AND SO I JUST GAVE—

A LITTLE SONG AND DANCE INSTEAD.

WELL, I'VE JUST REMEMBERED—

THAT IT WASN'T A DREAM!"

(1934)

GIOVANNETTI

(1953)

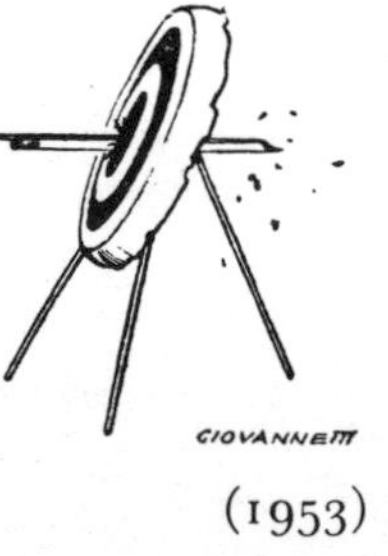

(1953)

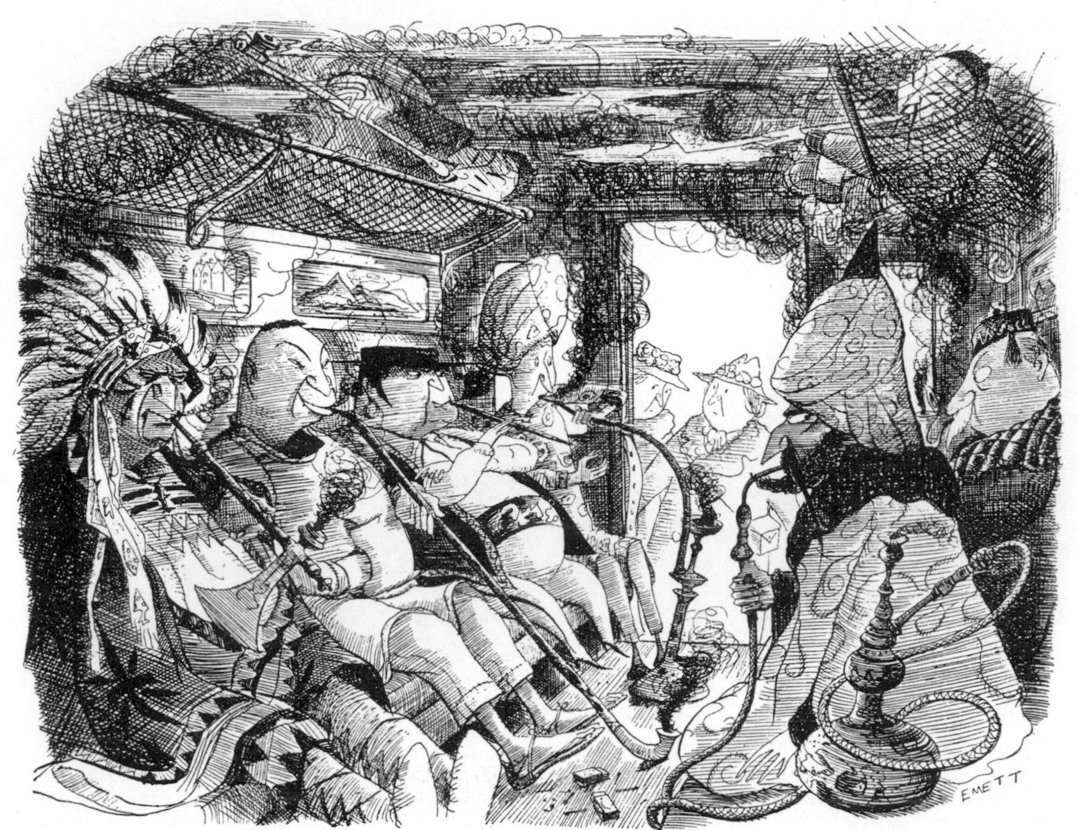

"Bother—it's a smoker!"
(1942)

"So they're not going to be bungalows after all."
(1947)

"I ~~*still*~~ *reckon we should 'ave been the 8.35 to the City!"*
(1943)

(1954)

(1951)

(1946)

"Flyovers, motorways, and such! What's the matter with the roads we've got?"
(1955)

(1951)

"*Yes, it's supposed to act as a sort of safety valve, otherwise they'd all be sittin' at home or goin' to the pictures, or somethin'.*"

(1945)

(1952)

(1952)

"Hundreds of pounds on window displays, and all they do is shove a couple of pups in theirs."

(1951)

"*I shouldn't eat that, sir—it's just possible that it's part of the ceiling.*"

(1952)

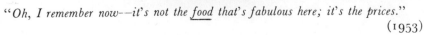

"*Oh, I remember now—it's not the* food *that's fabulous here; it's the prices.*"

(1953)

"Last year it was seaweed flies."
(1954)

"A fine time to tell me now that someone's thought of it already."
(1953)

(1949)

J. W. TAYLOR

(1950)

"It's a must."
(1953)

"To think I married you because you were such fun."
(1954)

"Back to the old brain-washing again, I suppose."
(1953)

"You see, Mr. Carlo, there's nothing really sensational about your act—I can do it myself."

(1947)

"Lady Gilpin's just going, Charles."

(1954)

"For instance—obviously you haven't done under this bed."

(1946)

"Could I change it? I find my husband already has one."

(1949)

(1955)

(1951)

(1951)

(1954)

"We're giving you a larger district, Johnson."
(1955)

"How can I convince you that I'm genuinely sorry?"
(1953)

"Ah well, it takes all sorts to make the world."
(1952)

"My first husband wouldn't have stumbled while he was carrying me."

(1955)

"And let's hope this teaches you that crime doesn't pay."

(1946)

"My mistake, speaking as an ex-cashier of the Metropolitan Bank, lay in not returning to the scene of the crime."

(1952)

"Now what happened?—tell us in your own words."

(1953)

NORMAN MANSBRIDGE

"Pot of tea for two—Indian or China?"

(1946)

(1951)

(1952)

(1954)

Eric Burgin

(1954)

"There goes a car with exactly the same number as ours."

(1952)

(1951)

"Worst organized stampede I ever attended."
(1952)

"You can tell the ones that are hand made."
(1954)

"But I don't <u>know</u> the people upstairs."

(1953)

(1953)

(1950)

"We can manage without a maid now, but I don't know where we'd be without him."

(1951)

"What's happened to the girl who was here yesterday?"

(1953)

ONE FOR THE ROAD

At the punch-bowl's brink
Let the thirsty think
  What they say in Japan:
"First the man takes a drink,
Then the drink takes a drink,
  Then the drink takes the man!"

E. R. SILL 1883

There are two reasons for drinking: one is, when you are thirsty, to cure it; the other, when you are not thirsty, to prevent it. . . . Prevention is better than cure.

T. LOVE PEACOCK 1817

One for the road
(1947)

A DAY AT THE CAMP

Sentinel: "WHO COMES THERE?"
Ebriosus: "FRIEND!"
Sentinel: "ADVANCE, FRIEND!"
Ebriosus: "ADVANSH! COME, THATSH A GOOD UN!"

(1860)

Ticket Collector: "NOW, THEN, MAKE HASTE! WHERE'S YOUR TICKET?"
Bandsman (refreshed): "AU'VE LOST IT!"
Ticket Collector: "NONSENSE! FEEL IN YOUR POCKETS. YE CANNOT HEV LOST IT!"
Bandsman: "AW CANNOT?! WHY, MAN, AU'VE LOST THE BIG DRUM!"

(1871)

Young Wife (2 A. M.): "DINNER AT THE ALBION! THE THEATRE! AND SUPPER AND A RUBBER AT THE CLUB! WELL, HENRY, I WONDER YOU DID NOT GO TO ALL THE PLACES OF AMUSEMENT IN LONDON, AND (*sobbing*) NOT COME HOME ALL NIGHT!"

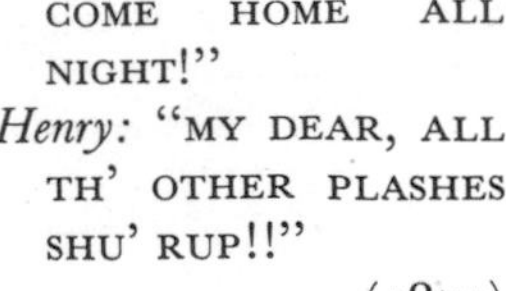

Henry: "MY DEAR, ALL TH' OTHER PLASHES SHU' RUP!!"

(1871)

OVERDOING IT

Minister (to one of his flock): "I'M SHOC ED, JAMES, TO SEE YOU'VE BROK YOUR PROMISE AND HAVE BEEN DULGING AGAIN." (*James hangs head.*) "YOU REALLY SHOULD GIVE UP. IT DOES YOU GREAT HARM MAKES YOU UNFIT FOR WORK—SPO YOUR APPEARANCE—YE CANNA T YER BREAKFAST—YE'VE A BAD TA I' YER MOOTH—GIVES YE A SPLETT HEADACHE—"
James: "A-YE, MENESTER! BUT YE SUFFERED YERSEL'!"

(18

VINOUS LOGIC

Respectable Pawnbroker (roused from his at 3 A.M. by repeated Knockings at h "WELL! WHAT IS IT?"
Ebriosus: "WHATSH THE TIME?"
Respectable Pawnbroker: "WHAT! DO Y TO SAY YOU'VE GOT ME OUT OF BED TIME O' NIGHT TO ASK ME SUCH QUESTION AS THAT?—POLICE! P
Ebriosus: "WELL, HANG IT, GOVERNOR —YOU'VE GOT MY WATCH."

Priest: "YOU DRUNKEN SOT! THE VERY BEASTS OF THE FIELD GIVE YOU A LESSON! THEY LEAVE OFF WHEN THEY HAVE QUENCHED THEIR THIRST."
Paddy: "YES, YER RIV'RENCE. BUT WHERE DID THE BASTES IVER COME ACRASS A STHRAME O' WHISKEY!!?"
(1879)

Doctor (who had just seen the Patient): "HE'S NO WORSE, BUT" *(gravely)* "THE QUESTION WILL, NO DOUBT, SOON ARISE AS TO THE ADVISABILITY OF TAPPING HIM."
Mother-in-law: "OH, DOCTOR, DON'T SAY THAT! NOTHING WAS EVER TAPPED IN THIS HOUSE THAT LASTED OVER A WEEK!!"
(1880)

n (sternly): "HOW COULD YOU ME TO CHURCH TO BE MAR- D TO A MAN IN SUCH A STATE THAT!"
(weeping): "IT WASN'T MY ULT, SIR. I NEVER CAN GET TO COME WHEN HE'S ER!!"
(1878)

Gentleman of Leisure: "YOU DON'T SAY YOU'VE STARTED WORK, JOE? THIS IS THE FIRST STROKE I'VE SEEN YE DO SINCE I'VE KNOWN YE."
Joe: "ITS THE FIRST JOB I'VE EVER FOUND AS I COULD PUT ME 'EART IN."
(1908)

Pat (giving the Squire "Notice"): "WHAT DID WE AGREE WHIN I TUK THE PLACE?—THAT WE SHOULD NIVER BE DRUNK AT THE SAME TOIME!—BUT FAIX YE NIVER GI' ME THE CHANCE!!"
(1878)

MORAL!

NEAT AND TIDY!

TIGHT AND NEEDY!
(1884)

Officer (to Native Servant): "WHAT CASTE ARE YOU, RAMJAMMER?"
Oriental: "SAME RELIGION AS SAHIB. DRINK BRANDY, SAR!!"
(1874)

THE WONDERS OF SCIENCE

The Principal (from the City, through the Telephone, to the Foreman at the "Works"): "HOW DO YOU GET ON, PAT?"

Irish Foreman (in great awe of the instrument): "VERY WELL, SIR. THE GOODS IS SENT OFF."

The Principal (knowing Pat's failing): "WHAT HAVE YOU GOT TO DRINK THERE?"

Pat (startled): "OCH! LOOK AT THAT NOW! IT'S ME BREATH THAT DONE IT!"

(1881)

Sentry: "'OO GOES THERE?"

Jock: "TWA SCOTCHES, AN' AWFU' UNDER PROOF."

(1917)

Bibulous Binks: "GAD, IT'S FREEZING AGAIN!"

(1901)

Nervous Tourist: "ARE YOU SURE THE DRIVER IS A STRICTLY SOBER MAN? HE DOES NOT LOOK LIKE AN ABSTAINER."

Landlord: "WEEL, THERE'S NO AN ABSTAINER ABOOT THE PLACE, MAM, BUT HE'S THE NEXT BEST THING TAE IT; YE CANNA FILL THAT ONE FULL."

(1913)

Magistrate: "YOU ARE CHARGED WITH HAVING BEEN DRUNK WHEN IN CHARGE OF A CHILD UNDER THE AGE OF SEVEN YEARS."

Prisoner: "PLEASE, YOUR WORSHIP, SHE WAS A-TAKIN' ME 'OME."

(1903)

Tourist: "HAVE YOU NOT GOT SCOTCH WHISKEY?"
Waiter (in an Irish Hotel): "NO, SORR, WE DON'T KAPE IT. AND THEM AS DOES ONLY USES IT TO WATER DOWN OUR OWN!"

(1902)

Officer: "WHEN YOU SEE A MOON LIKE THAT, THOMPSO DOESN'T IT SOMETIMES MAKE YOU FEEL A LITTLE SENTIMENTAL?"
P.O.: "NO, SIR, I CAN'T SAY IT DO, THE ON'Y TIMI GETS SLOPPY NOW IS WHEN I'VE 'AD A FEW NIC LOOKIN' PINTS O' BEER."

(192

FROM AN X-RAY PHOTOGRAPH TAKEN RECENTLY IN AMERICA

(1923)

New York Tailor: "ABOUT THE HIP POCKET, SIR—PINT OR HALF-PINT?"

(1922)

(1945)

"WELL, ONE OF US MUST BE WRONG."

(1938)

"WELL, I'VE TRIED MOST THINGS AN' BIN IN PUBS ALL OVER THE WORLD IN MY SEARCH FOR 'UMAN 'APPINESS AN' I'VE COME TO THE CONCLUSION THAT IT DON'T EXIST."
"NO, BUT THE PUBS DOES."

(1935)

"Not just now for me, thanks. I have to drive."
(1946)

"Not for me, thanks, I'm driving."
(1954)

(1950)

(1949)

"He only drinks to be sociable."
(1946)

(1954)

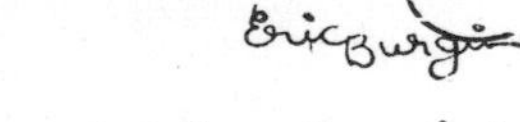

"I don't usually drink this amount, but I've got my foot trapped."

(1952)

"Boy! What a party!"

(1952)

THE SEAMY SIDE

"Despayre not, though fortune be contrary
for her wheele doth alwayes turn about."

JOHN FLORIO 1578

GOOD ADVERTISEMENT

"I USED YOUR SOAP TWO YEARS AGO; SINCE THEN I HAVE USED NO OTHER."

(1884)

ANOTHER BIT FROM THE MINING DISTRICTS

First: "WU'T TAK THY QUOAT OFF, THEN? OI TELL THEE OI'M AS GOOD A MON AS THEE!"
Second: "THEE A MON! WHOY THEE BE'ST ONLY WALKIN' ABOUT TO SAVE THY FUNERAL EXPENSES!"

(1854)

FURTHER ILLUSTRATION OF THE MINING DISTRICTS

First Polite Native: "WHO'S 'IM, BILL?"
Second ditto: "A STRANGER!"
First ditto: " 'EAVE 'ARF A BRICK AT 'IM!"

(1854)

SCENE — WESTMINSTER BRIDGE. TIME—TWO ON A FOGGY MORNING

Reduced Tradesman (to little party returning home): "DID YOU WANT TO BUY A GOOD RAZOR?"

(1853)

WHAT NEXT INDEED!

Grateful Recipient: "BLESS YOU, MY LADY! MAY WE MEET IN HEAVEN!"
Haughty Donor: "GOOD GRACIOUS!! DRIVE ON, JARVIS!!!"
(*She had evidently read Dr. Johnson, who "didn't want to meet certain people anywher*

(18

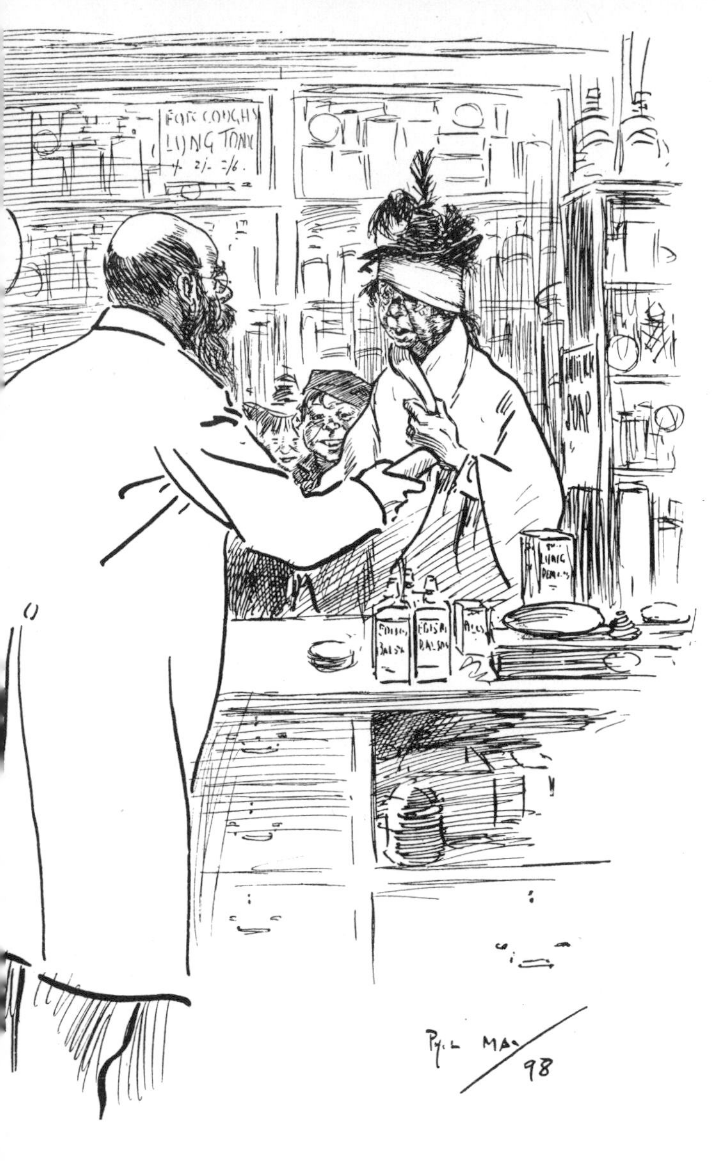

Chemist (to battered female, who is covered with scratches): "THE CAT, I SUPPOSE?"
Battered Female: "NO, ANOTHER LYDY!"

(1898)

'HOW DID YOU COME TO BEAT YOUR WIFE?"
'SOOPERIOR FOOTWORK."

(1934)

MAKING "A CLEAN BREAST OF IT"

Softhearted Old Lady (when she'd heard the Story and assisted Applicant): "DEAR ME! AH, POOR MAN! YOU MUST INDEED HAVE GONE THROUGH DREADFUL TRIALS."
Tramp: "I B'LIEVE YER, M'UM!—AN' WHAT'S WUS, M'UM, I WAS AL'AYS CONVICTED!"

(1887)

"WOT CHEER, ALF? YER LOOKIN' SICK; WOT IS IT?"
"WORK! NUFFINK BUT WORK, WORK, WORK, FROM MORNIN' TILL NIGHT."
" 'OW LONG 'AVE YER BEEN AT IT?"
"START TOMORRER."

(1911)

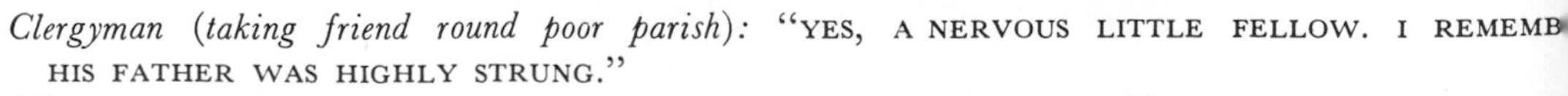

Clergyman (taking friend round poor parish): "YES, A NERVOUS LITTLE FELLOW. I REMEMB HIS FATHER WAS HIGHLY STRUNG."
Woman: "YE REMEMBER WRONG, THEN. 'E GOT ORF WIV TEN YEARS!"

(19

Accused (just dismissed): "MANY THANKS! WHAT SHOULD I HAVE DONE WITHOUT YOU?"
Counsel: "OH, ABOUT SIX MONTHS."
(1920)

Kindhearted Gentleman: "WHAT'S THE MATTER WITH YOUR HEAD?"
Guttersnipe: "FARVER."
Kindhearted Gentleman: "WHERE'S YOUR FATHER?"
Guttersnipe: " 'ORSPITAL."
Kindhearted Gentleman: "ACCIDENT?"
Guttersnipe: "NO, MUVVER!"
(1912)

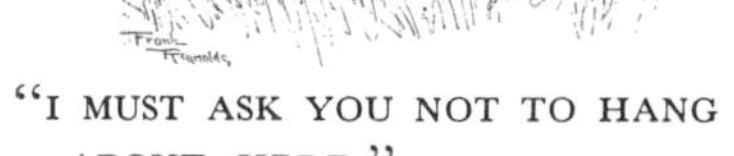

"I MUST ASK YOU NOT TO HANG ABOUT HERE."
"AND 'OO MIGHT YOU BE?
"I'M THE SECRETARY OF THIS CLUB."
"OH, ARE YER? WELL, THAT AIN'T THE WAY TO GET MEMBERS."
(1923)

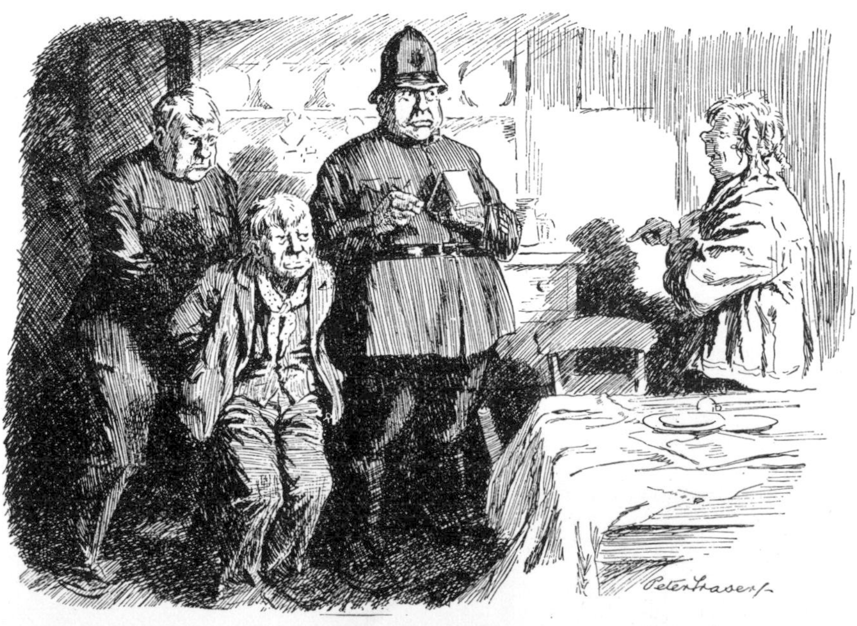

SITUATION: *Burglar caught red-handed.*
Woman: "THE SORCE O' THE FELLER! 'E PRETENDED TO BE MY 'USBAND AND CALLED OUT, 'IT'S ALL RIGHT, DARLIN'—IT'S ONLY ME.' IT WAS THE WORD 'DARLIN' ' WOT GIVE 'IM AWAY."
(1920)

Stout Lady: "IT'S LOVELY, AIN'T IT, SIR?"
Vicar: "LOVELY! WHAT IS LOVELY?"
Stout Lady: "WHY, THE BACK-TALK WOT SHE GIVES 'IM."

(1928)

P.C.: "YOUR 'USBAND WON'T BE 'OME TONIGHT, MISSUS. WE'VE JUST RUN 'IM IN."
Lidy: "WELL, YOU KNOWS YOUR OWN BUSINESS BEST. I'VE JUST RUN 'IM AHT."

(1929)

VELL, CLEVER! HAVING MADE OUR ESCAPE TO THE ROOF, WHAT DO WE DO NEXT?"

(1934)

THE ONLY ONE WE BELIEVE

Man who has drawn a runner in the Irish Sweep (to reporter): "PUT DAHN AS 'OW, IF I WIN, IT WON'T MAKE NO DIFFERENCE TO MY WAY O' LIFE."

(1932)

IN THE FAMILY

Visitor: "IF YOU DON'T BUZZ OFF, I'LL CALL THAT POLICEMAN."
The Pest: "HA! HA! DAT PLEECEMAN NO DAM GOOD. 'E MY BRUDDER."

(1932)

"Two requests—one for you to play Ravel's "Bolero," and the other for you to get the blazes out of here."

(1948)

JEWELLERS

JEWELLERS

JEWELLERS

JEWELLERS

JEWELLERS

JEWELLERS

(1951)

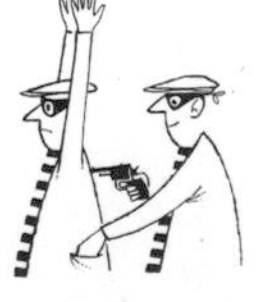

"WHAT'S A PARASITE, ALF?"
"SEARCH ME."

(1932)

"He isn't in; could I take a message?"
(1953)

(1954)

But, when the wit began to wheeze
And wine had warmed the politician
Cur'd yesterday of my disease
I died last night of my physician.

MATTHEW PRIOR

BEDSIDE MANNERISMS

If one compares the doctor and patient jokes of today with those of yesteryear there is a difference. In the old days the joke was against the doctor, today it is against the patient. Does this mean that there are fewer chinks in the medicos' armour these days?

The psychiatrist's couch is now a stock gag and can be said to have come of age now that the picture need not bear the psychiatrist's certificate on the wall. The inference from the trend of jokes is that as the doctor has become surer of himself the patient has become more and more a bundle of neuroses and complexes.

It is interesting to note that the term "bedside manner" originated with the first drawing on the next page.

". . . and keep him in bed another day or two."
(1950)

ANNALS OF A WINTER HEALTH RESORT

Lady Visitor: "OH, THAT'S YOUR DOCTOR, IS IT? WHAT SORT OF A DOCTOR IS HE?"

Lady Resident: "OH, WELL, I DON'T KNOW MUCH ABOUT HIS ABILITY; BUT HE'S GOT A VERY GOOD BEDSIDE MANNER!"

(1884)

THE NEW DOCTOR

"THE HIDEAR OF A YOUNG MAN LIKE THAT A-TELLING O' ME 'OW POOR PEOPLE'S CHILDREN HOUGHTER BE FED AND LOOKED AFTER! WHY, I'VE BURIED FOURTEEN O' MY OWN!"

(1893)

Shepherd (concluding tale of bereavement): "SAE A GIED HER SOME O' THAT WEE BOTTLE THAT YE LEFT YEST'RE'EN, AN' SHE JUST SLIPPIT AWA' AT FOWER O'CLOCK THE MORN."

Doctor: "DEAR, DEAR! I'M VERY SORRY TO HEAR THAT."

Shepherd (thoughtfully): "EH, MAN DOCTOR, ISNA IT A MAIRCY A DIDNA TAK' ANY O' THE WEE BOTTLE MASEL'!"

(1908)

First Doctor: "I ORDERED HIM AN ICE-COLD BATH EVERY MORNING."

Second Doctor: "WHAT, WHEN HE HAD INFLUENZA!"

First Doctor: "YES. IT WILL GIVE HIM PNEUMONIA, AND I MADE MY WHOLE REPUTATION CURING THAT!"

(1896)

Doctor: "WELL, JOHN, HOW ARE YOU TODAY?"
John: "VERRA BAD, VERRA BAD. I WISH PROVIDENCE 'UD 'AVE MUSSY ON ME AN' TAKE ME!"
Wife: " 'OW CAN YOU EXPECT IT TO IF YOU WON'T TAKE THE DOCTOR'S PHYSIC?"

(1905)

WONDERFUL EFFECTS OF ETHER
N A CASE OF SCOLDING WIFE

Patient: "THIS IS REALLY QUITE DELIGHTFUL—A MOST BEAUTIFUL DREAM."

(1847)

First Lady Doctor: "HE IS SLEEPING NOW, AND IS CERTAINLY RECOVERING. HE PROPOSED TO ME THIS MORNING."
Second Lady Doctor: "INDEED! HE WAS PROBABLY DELIRIOUS."

(1907)

Fleet Surgeon: "THERE DOESN'T SEEM MUCH WRONG WITH YOU, MY MAN. WHAT'S THE MATTER?"

A.B.: "WELL, SIR, IT'S LIKE THIS, SIR. I EATS WELL AN' I DRINKS WELL, AN' I SLEEPS WELL; BUT WHEN I SEES A JOB OF WORK—THERE, I'M ALL OF A TREMBLE!"

(1898)

DIAGNOSED

Patient: "I'M FEELING WRETCHED, DOCTOR. I TAKE NO INTEREST IN ANYTHING, HAVE NO APPETITE, CAN'T SLEEP—"

Doctor: "WHY DON'T YOU MARRY THE GIRL?"

(1898)

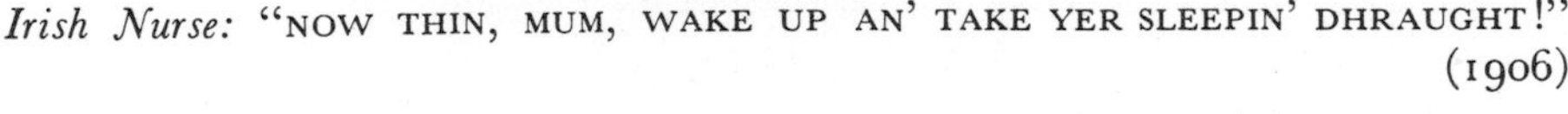

Irish Nurse: "NOW THIN, MUM, WAKE UP AN' TAKE YER SLEEPIN' DHRAUGHT!"

(1906)

INTELLIGENT ANTICIPATION

Fougasse

"H'M, YES—I FEAR WE MUST KNOCK OFF TOBACCO."
"CERTAINLY. I NEVER SMOKE."

"AND ALCOHOL ALSO, I'M AFRAID."
"BY ALL MEANS. I'M A TEETOTALER."

"STRONG TEA AND COFFEE ARE EQUALLY POISONOUS, BEAR IN MIND."
"RATHER. I NEVER TOUCH THEM."

"NO SUGAR OR SWEET THINGS, REMEMBER!"
"EXCELLENT! I DETEST 'EM."

"A MEAT DIET STRICTLY FORBIDDEN."
"SPLENDID. I'M A VEGETARIAN."

"A COLD BATH EVERY MORNING!!!"
"GLORIOUS. I ALWAYS HAVE ONE."

"AND G-GO AWAY FOR A LONG BRACING CHANGE TO THE B-BLEAKEST PART OF THE EAST COAST!!!!"
"PRICELESS! WHY, MY DEAR OLD FELLOW—

I LIVE THERE!"

(1922)

Sailor: "IT'S A REMARKABLE THING, SIR, BUT WHEN I WOGGLES ME LEG LIKE THIS I GETS A 'ORRIBLE PAIN IN IT."
Irritable Ship's Doctor: "THEN WHY THE ——— DO YOU DO IT?"

(1928)

Doctor: "WHAT DID YOU OPERATE ON JONES FOR?"
Surgeon: "A HUNDRED POUNDS."
Doctor: "NO, I MEAN WHAT HAD HE GOT?"
Surgeon: "A HUNDRED POUNDS."

(1925)

HORRORS OF THE GREEN

OUR DENTIST FAILS TO FILL A CAVITY.

(1921)

". . . AND THE DOCTORS ALL SAID THEY'D NEVER SEEN ONE LIKE IT."

(1937)

REJUVENATION

(1925)

First Doctor (referring to millionaire patient): "HE WILL RECOVER."
Second Ditto: "I THINK SO TOO. WE HAVE GOT OVER THE WORST."
First Ditto: "NO. THE WORST IS YET TO COME. WE HAVE TO INFORM THE RELATIVES."

(1933)

"Like a heavy weight pressing on your stomach—eh?"

(1948)

Lady (who has brought her boy to the hospital): "IT'S 'IS 'EAD, NURSE. 'E'S 'AD IT OFF AN ON EVER SINCE 'E WAS BORN."

(193

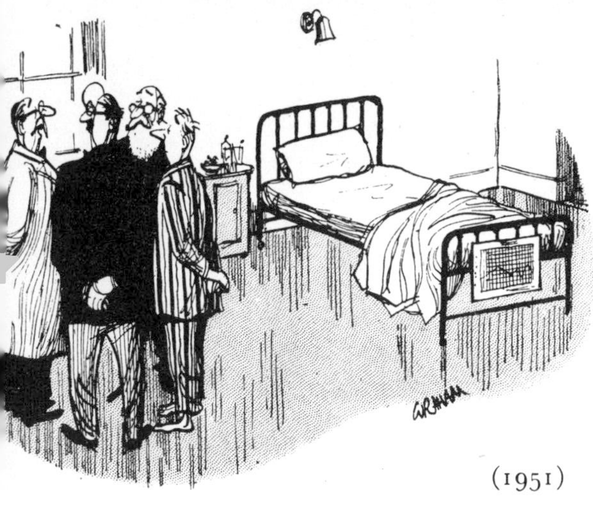

(1951)

"Good morning, Mrs. Todhunter. How's the inferiority complex?"

(1944)

"Well, to start with——I was rather shy as a boy . . ."

(1950)

(1948)

"Don't worry, there's nothing wrong with your husband that your kind nursing and someone else's cooking can't cure."

(1947)

"Tell me more about this kleptomaniac tendency, Mrs. Henderson."
(1952)

FOR THE DURATION . . .

The effect of war on the citizen, either in or out of uniform, has proved a mine (self-detonating) of humour, and no excuses are offered for devoting so long a section to it.

Hitler's looks were a "natural" for the comic artist in World War II as were the blackout and the friendly invasion of Britain by American troops. Without these aids in World War I, the joking was narrower in aim and closer to the trenches. Despite this, the comment with the picture below applies to the humour, too—and is no disparagement at that.

"The old place hasn't changed a bit from 1917!"

(1945)

Captain: "WHAT'S THE CHARGE, SERGEANT?"
Sergeant: "THIS TIME IT'S DRUNKENNESS, SIR. BUT THIS MAN IS THE MOST TROUBLESOME FELLOW IN THE REGIMENT, SIR. HE GOES OUT WHEN HE LIKES, AND COMES IN WHEN HE LIKES, AND GETS DRUNK WHEN HE LIKES—IN FACT, HE MIGHT BE A HORFICER!!"
(1880)

MILITARY EDUCAT

General: MR. DE BRIDOON, WHA IS THE GENERAL USE OF CA ALRY IN MODERN WARFARE?
Mr. de Bridoon: "WELL, I SU POSE TO GIVE TONE TO WHA WOULD OTHERWISE BE A MER VULGAR BRAWL!"
(189

Old Gentleman (Military man, guest of the Squire's, conversing with smart-looking Rustic): "WOUNDED IN THE CRIMEA WERE YOU? BADLY?
Rustic: "THE BULLET HIT ME IN THE CHIST, HERE, SURR, AN' CAME OUT AT ME BACK!"
Old Gentleman: "THE DEUCE! COME, COME, PAT, THAT WON'T DO! WHY, IT WOULD HAVE GONE RIGHT THROUGH YOUR HEART, MAN!"
Rustic: "OCH, FAIX ME HEART WAS IN ME MOUTH AT THE THOIME, SURR!!"
(1881)

A DILEMMA

Auxiliary Recruit (to himself): "MURDER! MURDER! WHAT'LL I DO NOW? 'DRILL-TOULD ME ALWAYS TO SALUTE ME OFFICER WID THE FAR-OFF HAND, AND HER IV EM! FAIX, I'LL MAKE IT STRAIGHT FOR MESELF ANYHOW!" (*Throws up bot*

Irascible Lieutenant (down engine-room tube): "IS THERE A BLITHERING IDIOT AT THE END OF THIS TUBE?"
Voice from Engine-room: "NOT AT AT THIS END, SIR!"

(1898)

Murphy: "WHIN THE WHARR'S OVER, I THINK THERE'LL BE A CONSCRIPCHUN."
Clancy: "NO! THERE'LL BE NO CONSCRIPCHUN. BUT I THINK THEY'LL FOORCE IVERY WAN IV US TO BE VOLENTEERS!"

(1900)

"WHATEVER HAVE YOU BEEN DOING WITH YOURSELF, MURPHY? YOU LOOK ALL BROKEN UP!"
"WELL, YER 'ANNER, I WINT TO WAN IV THIM 'SHTOP-THE-WAR' MEETINGS LASHT NOIGHT!"

(1900)

nergetic Sub has been pursuing naway Mule. "WELL DONE, OLD CHAP! YOU DESERVE THE D.S.O. AT LEAST. WHAT IS IT? AMMUNITION?"
MMUNITION! D.S.O.!! V.C., YOU MEAN!!!! WHY, IT'S BOTTLED BEER!!!!"

(1900)

FORE AND ——

Sergeant: "BACK A LITTLE, NUMBER FIVE!"

——AFT

Sergeant: "UP A LITTLE, NUMBER FIVE!"

(1903)

DEEDS THAT OUGHT TO WIN THE V. C.

THE PRIVATE GROWS A BETTER MU
TACHE THAN THE SERGEANT.

(191

Adjutant (discovering second button of tunic unfastened): "DASH IT AI
SERGEANT-MAJOR! HERE'S A FELLAH HALF NAKED! MAKE HIM
PRIZ'NAR!"

(190

WAY THEY HAVE IN THE ARMY

Sergeant (preparing a squad for church parade): "RECRUITS! 'SHUN! THOSE AS CAN READ WILL FOLLOW THE REGLASHUNS. THOSE AS CAN'T READ WILL GO THROUGH THE REQUISITE MOTIONS, AS FOLLOWS:— ONE! EXTEND LEFT 'AND 'OLDING PRAYER BOOK. TWO! RAISE RIGHT 'AND TO LEVEL OF MOUTH. THREE! MOISTEN THUMB O' RIGHT 'AND. FOUR! TURN HOVER PAGE!"

(1907)

unctilious Officer: "DON'T YOU KNOW THAT YOU MUST SALUTE AN OFFICER?"

ecruit: "YES, SIR; BUT I WAS TOLD NEVER TO DO IT WITH A PIPE IN MY MOUTH."

(1915)

Instructor: "GO ON! KILL IT! YOU DON'T COME HERE TO BE LEARNT TATTOOIN'."

(1918)

A WORLD OF SHAMS

Officer (of Umpire Staff): "HI, YOU THERE! YOU MUSTN'T CROSS HERE! CAN'T YOU SEE THE NOTICE? THIS BRIDGE IS SUPPOSED TO BE DESTROYED."

Subaltern (cheerfully): "OH, THAT'S ALL RIGHT! WE'RE SUPPOSED TO BE SWIMMING ACROSS."

(1910)

Tommy (dictating letter to be sent to his wife): "THE NURSES HERE ARE A VERY PLAIN LOT—

Nurse: "OH, COME! I SAY! THAT'S NOT VERY POLITE TO US."

Tommy: "NEVER MIND, NURSE, PUT IT DOWN. IT'LL PLEASE HER!"

(1916)

Visitor (at private hospital): "CAN I SEE LIEUTENANT BARKER, PLEASE?"

Matron: "WE DO NOT ALLOW ORDINARY VISITING. MAY I ASK IF YOU'RE A RELATIVE?"

Visitor (boldly): "OH, YES! I'M HIS SISTER."

Matron: "DEAR ME! I'M VERY GLAD TO MEET YOU. I'M HIS MOTHER."

(1916)

Tommy: "NOW THEN, HANDS UP, OR YOU'RE A DEAD MAN."

(1916)

OUR AMAZON CORPS "STANDING EASY"

(1916)

"I HEAR YOU'VE GOT A BERTH IN THE WAR OFFICE. IS IT HARD WORK?"

"NOT AFTER YOU GET IT."

(1916)

Wounded Soldier: "ALL THE 'UNS AIN'T COWARDS, MISS. WHY, SIX ON 'EM CAME FOR OLD MAC HERE, AND IT WAS A LONG TIME AFORE THEY GIVE IN."

(1916)

WAR'S BRUTALIZING INFLUENCE

FASHION PLATE—OLD STYLE
FASHION PLATE—NEW STYLE

Orderly Officer: "WHAT ARE YOU DOING WITHOUT YOUR RIFLE, SENTRY?"
Tommy: "BEG PARDON, SIR, BUT I AIN'T THE SENTRY."
Orderly Officer: "WHO ARE YOU, THEN, AND WHERE IS THE SENTRY?"
Tommy: "OH, 'E'S INSIDE OUT OF THE RAIN. I'M ONE OF THE PRISONERS."

(1916)

Officer (with the M.E.F.): "NOW THEN, MY LAD, IF YOU CATCH HOLD OF HIS HEAD HE CAN'T KICK YOU."
Private: "NO, SIR. AND IF I CATCHES 'OLD OF THE BEGGAR'S TAIL 'E BLOOMIN' WELL CAN'T BITE ME."

(1916)

"WHAT THE DEVIL ARE YO
DOING DOWN THAT SHEL
HOLE? DIDN'T YOU HEA
ME SAY WE WERE O
AGAINST FOUR TO ONE
Geordie (a trade-unionist): "A
AA HEARD YOU; BUT AA'
KILLED MA FOWER."

(191

Corporal: "YOU NEEDN'T SAY A FOND GOOD-BYE TO THAT 'ORSE. YOU AIN'T SEEN THE LAST OF 'IM BY NO MEANS."

(1916)

Tommy (to Jock, on leave): "WHAT ABOUT THE LINGO? SUPPOSE YOU WANT AN EGG OVER THERE, WHAT DO YOU SAY?"
Jock: "YE JUIST SAY, 'OOF.' "
Tommy: "BUT SUPPOSE YOU WANT TWO?"
Jock: "YE SAY 'TWA OOFS, 'AND THE SILLY AULD FULE WIFE GIES YE THREE, AND YE JUIST GIE HER BACK ONE. MAN, IT'S AN AWFU' EASY LANGUAGE."

(1916)

C.O. (to sentry): "DO YOU KNOW THE DEFENCE SCHEME FOR THIS SECTOR OF THE LINE, MY MAN?"
Tommy: "YES, SIR."
C.O.: "WELL, WHAT IS IT, THEN?"
Tommy: "TO STAY 'ERE AN' FIGHT LIKE 'ELL."

(1917)

jor-General (addressing the men before practising an attack behind he lines): "I WANT YOU TO UNDERSTAND THAT THERE IS A IFFERENCE BETWEEN A REHEARSAL AND THE REAL THING. HERE ARE THREE ESSENTIAL DIFFERENCES: FIRST, THE ABENCE OF THE ENEMY. NOW *(turning to the Regimental Sergeant-Major)* WHAT IS THE SECOND DIFFERENCE?"
geant-Major: "THE ABSENCE OF THE GENERAL, SIR."

(1917)

Sergeant-Major: "FALL OUT, ANYONE THAT KNOWS ANYTHING ABOUT MOTORCARS." (Cadet falls out.) "NOW THEN, WHAT DO YOU KNOW ABOUT 'EM?"
Cadet: "WELL, SIR, I OWN A ROLLS-ROYCE."
Sergeant-Major: "OH, DO YOU? WELL, GO AND CLEAN THE ADJUTANT'S MOTORCYCLE."

(1916)

THE DREAM OF THE MAN OF FORTY-FIVE

HAVING TILLED THE SOIL FROM FIVE TO SEVEN EVERY MORNING,

CARRIED ON AT HIS OFFICE ALL DAY WITH A STAFF OF THREE INSTEAD OF THIRTY,

AND FULFILLED HIS DUTY AS A CITIZEN AT NIGHT,

HE IS PASSED INTO THE ARMY FOR "LIGHT GARRISON DUTY AT HOME." (1918)

Pet of the Platoon: "I DIDN'T HALF TELL OFF OUR SERGEANT JUST NOW. I CALLED HIM A KNOCK-KNEED, PIGEON-TOED, SWIVEL-EYED MONKEY, AND SAID HE OUGHT TO GO TO A NIGHT SCHOOL!"
Ecstatic Chorus: "AND WHAT DID HE SAY?"
Bill (after a pause): "WELL, AS A MATTER OF FAC', I DON'T THINK HE QUITE HEARD ME."

(1917)

THE RECRUIT'S FAREWELL TO THE BOWLER

(1917)

"DIDN'T KNOW WOT 'APPINESS WAS TILL I GOT MARRIED."

"AND NOW YOU'VE 'AD TO LEAVE IT, EH?"

"WOTCHER MEAN, LEAVE IT? I'VE COME BACK TO IT."

(1917)

Sergeant-Major (who has the professional mind): "HE'S A GOOD MAN IN THE TRENCHES, SIR, AND A GOOD MAN IN A SCRAP, SIR; BUT YOU'LL NEVER MAKE A SOLDIER OF HIM."

(1917)

"WELL, JACK! HERE'S GOOD NEWS FROM HOME. WE'RE TO HAVE A MEDAL."
"THAT'S VERY KIND. MAYBE ONE OF THESE DAYS WE'LL HAVE A COAT TO STICK IT ON?"

(1856)

Awe-struck Tommy (from the trenches): "LOOK, BILL —— SOLDIERS!"

(1917)

Gretchen: "WILL IT NEVER END? THINK OF OUR AWFUL RESPONSIBILITY BEFORE HUMANITY."
Hans: "AND THESE EVERLASTING SARDINES FOR EVERY MEAL."

(1917)

BERLIN OFFICIAL

"GOOD NEWS AGAIN THIS MORNING."
"ACH! I GROW WEARY OF GOOD NEWS."
"COME, COME, MY FRIEND, WE MUST BE PATIENT AND BEAR THE SUCCESSES BRAVELY."

(1916)

Jones (left at home to mind the children): "IF THE PAPER'S ANYTHING TO GO BY, WE MARRIED MEN WILL ALL BE IN THE ARMY BY JULY. IT SEEMS A LONG TIME TO WAIT."

(1916)

THE INVENTOR'S DREAM

AN INEXPENSIVE IDEA FOR MAKING THE BRITISH ARMY INVULNERABLE

(1920)

(1920)

"Well, boys, I just got away from civilisation in time."

"My father says these things appear every twenty years." (1941)

"That's the sort of thing we try to discourage." (1937)

"You're Dummy, Mr. Bindlebine—see if that was *a small incendiary bomb."* (1939)

THE CHANGING FACE OF BRITAIN

1

2

(1940)

"Remember you used to say, Why must I wear that silly little hat perched on the side of my head and I used to say, Well, that's how they're worn?"

(1940)

"Get a move on——I've got a message countermanding yours."

(1940)

"Will you stop rustling that parachute!"

(1940)

"There are only the three regulars left now, Sir."
(1939)

"Dummy pops off and attacks the Docks at Brest ——O.K.?"
(1941)

"You mustn't expect us to do this every time you turn out improperly dressed."
(1940)

Uncle Frederic at 8.32 p.m. last Tuesday—if his description is strictly in accordance with the facts.

(1940)

"The new General is far more thorough in his inspections than the last one was."

(1939)

PROMOTION

(1941)

"Lucky? I'll say we were lucky!"
(1941)

"Pardon, Madam, I think we must have taken a wrong turning somewhere."
(1942)

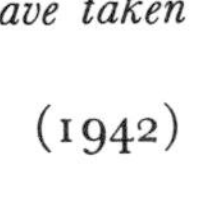

"*I'll thank you to take your orders from me and me only.*"

(1941)

"*Can't see a ruddy planet for Fortresses.*"

(1942)

can't imagine, Sergeant——unless it's a wishing-well."

(1941)

"*Come along, get moving, there's nothing difficult about it——I'm not asking you to do anything that I haven't done.*"

(1943)

". . . 'I remind you of who?' I said. And then I knocked the blighter down."

(1939)

"Of course it's a false one——but you'd be surprised at the number of jobs I get on the strength of it."

(1940)

"It says he done it all to save his face. Well, well."

(1939)

"Now, if we're going to put this over properly, you'll have to learn German."

(1940)

"*. . . I am beginning to think I have been letting things worry me too much lately, because . . .*"
(1938)

"*We won't waste time on Lincoln—he had some delusion about not being able to fool all the people.*"
(1940)

If one believed our contemporary humorists, one would get the impression that the civilian population spent its entire time——

waiting for buses that never stop——

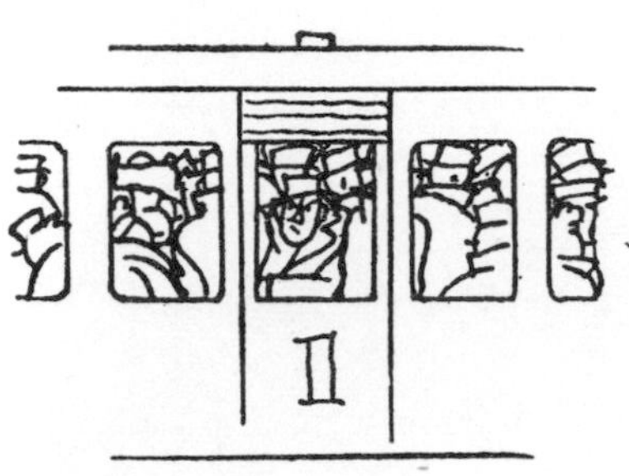

packed in trains that never arrive——

standing in queues that never get anything——

trying to get into hotels that are always full——

trying to hail taxis that are always engaged——

trying to rent flats that are always let——

trying to run offices that are always staffless——

trying to get warm in rooms that are always fireless——

and trying to run houses that are always maidless:

Now all this gives a very wrong impression: actually most of us still find plenty of time——

to sit comfortably at home and read all the latest books——

that, incidentally, are always out of print!!!!!!

(1944)

"Splendid! Splendid! You've almost got the hang of it."

(1941)

"Would you mind paying attention, Mrs. Eglethorpe, please? I hope you don't think they enclose directions with the bomb."

(1940)

"Calm yourself, dear. Even Hitler can't be both dregs and scum."

(1942)

"Actually this is now very much as Wren intended us to see St. Paul's."

(1941)

HIS USUAL SEAT
(1941)

"*Shall we join the ladies?*"
(1942)

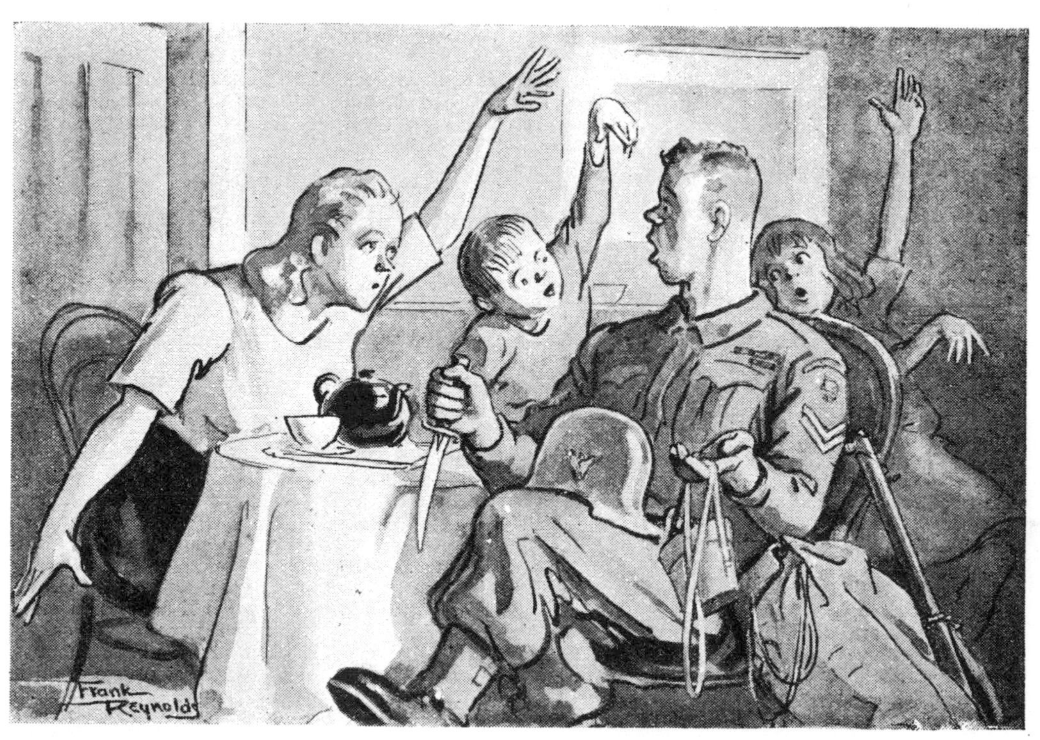

"*'Ere! 'Oo's supposed to be tellin' their experiences?*"
(1945)

(1940)

"*Well, I'm afraid you'll have to stay indoors, that's all.*"

(1939)

"*Well, it was your idea to have a black cat!*"

(1939)

"*Good evening, Madam. Over nine months ago—on the 3rd of September, 1939, to be precise—we declared war on Germany.*"

(1940)

"*Give him my compliments and tell him that, while we admire the subtlety of his point, we prefer to assume that the blackout regulations do <u>not</u> apply to searchlights.*"

(1940)

Orderly Sergeant: "LIGHTS OUT, THERE."
Voice from the Hut: "IT'S THE MOON, SERGINT."
Orderly Sergeant: "I DON'T GIVE A D——N WHAT IT IS. PUT IT OUT!"

(1918)

"19 Acacia Gardens still to come . . ."

(1940)

"Excuse me, but I think you should have got out the <u>other</u> side."

(1940)

"These war-time batteries are so <u>frightfully</u> weak!"

(1940)

"Gosh! Aren't you sick and tired of all these silly jokes about the black-out?"

(1939)

"*I tell ye, as sure as I'm from Dublin, and me name's Patrick O'Malley, old Ireland will stay neutral!*"
(1943)

"*There's that ant with the limp walking across the damn thing again.*"
(1944)

"*What made you go into the Navy instead of the coal mines?*"
(1943)

"Is it true that Hitler's going to invade us with five million men?"
"I hope so, Missus. If he doesn't I think I shall have to pop over and fetch him."
(1941)

. . . meanwhile, in Britain, the entire population, faced by the threat of invasion, has been flung into a state of complete panic . . ."
(1940)

"They won't let on who the camp is for."
(1942)

"Officer, how do we get to the native quarter?"
(1944)

"Gee, this is nothing——you ought t
have seen the way we imagined it ove
in the States."
(1942

"Dear Momma, in England they drive on the left side of the road. . ."

(1942)

"Ah, now YOU'll be able to direct me to Piccadilly Circus."

(1942)

". . . coming over to entertain the American troops, or something . . ."

(1943)

"Now I bet this makes you homesick for Dead Man's Gulch. . ."

(1944)

"It's all right—I expect they tell them that over here we drive on the left. . ."

(1944)

"Anyone from Texas on the train. . . ?"

(1944)

"They say, can we do two hundred and eighty-seven Dainty Afternoon Teas?"

(1944)

(1944)

"*Don't forget, Beryl— the response is 'hiya, fellers!' and a sort of nonchalant wave of the hand.*"
(1944)

"*Quite a little evening ceremony—Earl and Chester make Edwin a cup of tea and he makes them a mint julep.*" (1944)

(1944)

(1944)

"*Flight-Sergeant said 'Go and give 'em a hand in the cookhouse.' Trouble is I don't know the first thing about cooking.*"

(1943)

(1945)

"Here's another complaint about low flying from the local Archery Club."
(1944)

"Monsieur has reserved a table, yes?"
(1944)

"*P. S. I have grown a beard.*"

(1945)

"*Right! Now we've got that little lot off, what's the trouble with your bike?*"

(1944)

"*You won't 'arf cop it for being late for the invasion.*"

(1944)

(1951)

"The ceiling's Michelangelo, the decoration's Raphael, and the plumbing's Sapper Jones."

(1945)

(1945

(1946)

"But wasn't there someone *else* at El Alamein who could have saved your life?"

(1946)

"Before leaving, sir, may I take this opportunity of mentioning that I've noticed the efficient manner in which you go about your duties. In my organization, don't forget, sir, there's always an opening for a man like you as soon as you're released."

(1946)

"This week's subject for discussion is 'The World I Want After the War.' Would someone please prod Gunner Tomkins sharply in the ribs and ask him what sort of world he wants after the war."

(1944)

"I'd like to meet the bally confectioner who advised you to get our full month's ration of sweets all at once." (1942)

"It's such a relief to find someone who takes neither sugar NOR *milk— that* IS *right, isn't it, dear?"*

(1948)

"That's an emergency ration card, here's mummy in her first queue, this is a soap coupon. . ."

(1954)

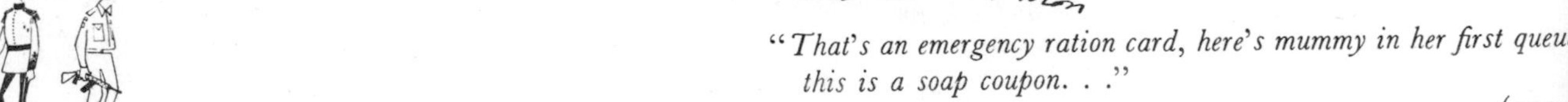

"*Tighten your belts, everybody, please—we're approaching Great Britain.*"

(1948)

"*But, my dear, we can't go on like this. It's three days since you mislaid the ration-books.*"

(1944)

"*Yes, I quite see that if only I had wrapped the pipes up with all the old clothes and blankets I haven't got, and kept up a roaring fire with all the coal I can't get, I shouldn't now be telephoning for the plumber that can't come.*"

"*How would you like your egg this month, dear?*"

(1944)

"*Are you ready to cut the cake, Madam?*" (1945)

"There should be some terrific car parks if they use the atom bomb."

(1947)

"See what I mean?"
(1947)

"Eureka!"
(1948)

TURNING THE PAGES

Here you can browse through cartoons on any and every subject with PUNCH's present-day artists in the majority.

MR. JOHN BULL AFTER AN ATTACK OF INCOME-TAX

(1847)

"It fought for years against rising taxation, but at last it surrendered."

(1946)

THE FALSE INCOME-TAX RETURN—

(1917)

CONTINUED OVER—

—AND ITS RECTIFICATION

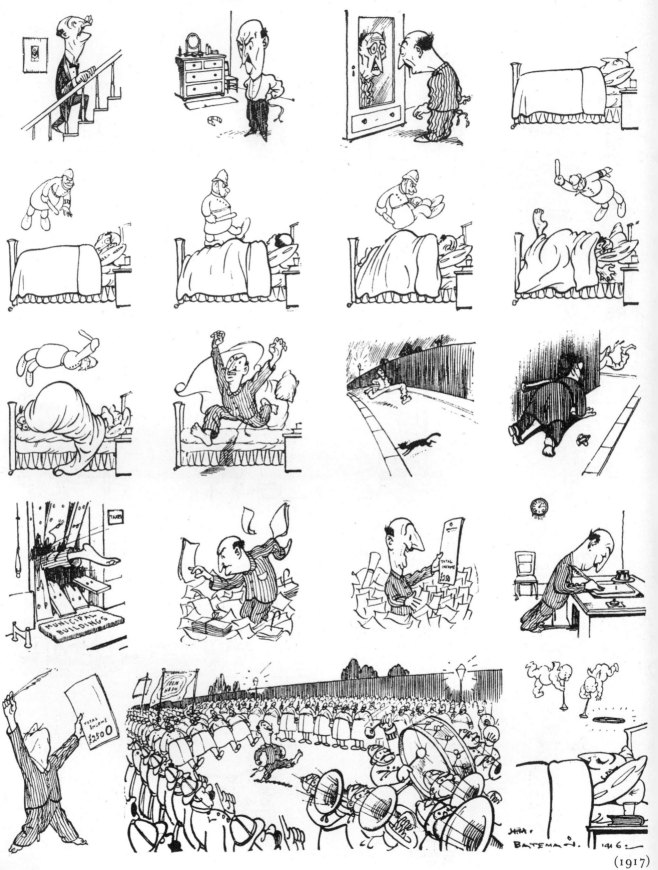

(1917)

FASHIONABLE MOVEMENTS

Street Dialogue

"*I'll punch yer ed, if yer say much.*"

"*Who'll punch my 'ed?*"

"*I will.*"

"*You will?*"

"*Yes, I will.*"

"*Well!—do it.*"

"*Ah!*"

"*Yes!*"

"*Oh!*"

(*Boys evaporate*) (1843)

The drawing above is the first bearing any resemblance to the modern captioned joke.

Nephew: "I HOPE YOU HAVEN'T BEEN WAITING LONG, UNCLE?"

Uncle: "ALL RIGHT, MY BOY. BEEN READING THE PAPER, AND HAD A PINCH—BY THE BYE, IT'S QUEER FLAVOURED SNUFF IN THIS JAR OF YOURS, FRED."

Nephew (aghast): "SNUFF, UNCLE!—JAR! GOOD GRACIOUS!—THAT'S NOT SNUFF! THOSE ARE THE ASHES OF MY LANDLORD'S FIRST WIFE!"

(1875)

My Lady: "I'M AFRAID I MUST GIVE UP THE PINEAPPLE, MR. GREEN! EIGHT SHILLINGS IN REALLY TOO MUCH!"

Successful Collier: "JUST PUT 'UN UP FOR ME, THEN, MASTER. 'ERE'S 'ARF A SOVEREIGN; AND LOOK 'ERE—YER MAY KEEP THE CHANGE IF YER'LL ONLY TELL US 'OW TO COOK 'UN!"

(1873)

THE DESCENT OF MAN

Figurative Party. "SO LONG AS I AM A MAN, SORR, WHAT DOES IT MATTER TO ME WHETHER ME GREAT-GRANDFATHER WAS AN ANTHROPOID APE OR NOT, SORR!"

Literal Party. "HAW! WATHER DISAGWEEABLE FOR YOUR GWATE GWANDMOTHER, WASN'T IT?" (1873)

Small but Sharp Passenger. "LOOK HERE! YOU DIDN'T GIVE ME THE RIGHT CHANGE JUST NOW!"

Clerk. "TOO LATE, SIR! YOU SHOULD HAVE SPOKEN WHEN YOU TOOK YOUR TICKET!"

Passenger. "SHOULD I? WELL, IT'S OF NO CONSEQUENCE TO ME; BUT YOU GAVE ME HALF-A-SOVEREIGN TOO MUCH! TA-TA!" [*Exit*

(1867)

AWFUL OCCURRENCE

Chorus of Unprotected Females. "CONDUCTOR! STOP! CONDUCTOR! OMNIBUS-MAN! HERE'S A GENTLEMAN HAD AN ACCIDENT AND BROKE A JAR OF LEECHES, AND THEY'RE ALL OVER THE OMNIBUS!" (1851)

Steward. "YOU CAN'T BE SICK HERE, SIR!" *Distressed Passenger.* "CAN'T I?" (*Is.*) (1912)

Militant Suffragist (*after long and futile efforts to light a fire for her tea-kettle*). "AND TO THINK THAT ONLY YESTERDAY I BURNT TWO PAVILIONS AND A CHURCH!" (1913)

First Sportsman (on the way home after dinner). "HI! LOOK OUT WHERE YOU'RE GOING!"

Second Sportsman. "LOOK OUT YOURSELF! YOU'RE DRIVING, AREN'T YOU?"

First Sportsman. "NO, I THOUGHT YOU WERE." (1914)

Workman (politely, to old Lady, who has accidentally got into a Smoking Compartment). "YOU DON'T OBJECT TO MY PIPE, I 'OPE, MUM?"

Old Lady. "YES, I DO OBJECT, VERY STRONGLY!"

Workman. "OH! THEN OUT YOU GET!"

(1895)

THE GUEST WHO WAS TOLD TO MAKE HIMSELF QUITE AT HOME, AND DID SO.

Policeman (making survey to investigate burglary): "IT'S EASY TO SEE THERE'S BEEN OLD HANDS AT WORK HERE, LADY."

Householder: "OH, THEY DIDN'T COME IN HERE. THIS IS MY DAUGHTER'S ROOM; SHE'S BEEN DRESSING FOR A DANCE."

(1932)

"EXCUSE ME, SIR, BUT ARE YOU READING THE PAPER YOU'RE SITTING ON?"

(1912)

Sister (to elderly prodigal who is much given to pawning his things): "WHAT'S THIS TICKET ON YER BEST COAT, SANDY?"
Sandy: "THAT WAS THE NICHT I WAS AT MCPHEARSON'S BALL, THEY TACK YER COAT FROM YE AT THE DOOR, AND GIE YE A TICKET FOR 'T."
Sister: "H'M—AYE—I SEE THERE'S ONE ON YER TROOSERS AS WELL."

(1909)

Solicitor: "NOW, AS A MATTER OF FACT, WHEN EXPRESSING YOUR OPINION OF YOUR OPPONENT, YOU DID USE A LEETLE STRONG LANGUAGE?"
Client: "WULL, I DON'T KNOW AS I FORGOT ANYTHING."

(1901)

Son: "I SAY, FATHER, HERE'S A CHANCE—AN ADVERTISEMENT OFFERING PERMANENT EMPLOYMENT TO A YOUNG MAN WILLING TO INVEST A HUNDRED POUNDS. I WONDER WHAT THE PERMANENT EMPLOYMENT IS."
Father: "TRYING TO GET THE HUNDRED POUNDS BACK."

(1923)

Urchin (to friend who has gone in): "B-I-I-LL! LEND US YER SKATES, YOU AIN'T USING 'EM!"

(1909)

"WHAT'S THE AVERAGE TIP THEY GIVE YOU FELLOWS?"

"'BOUT A DOLLAH, SAH."

"THERE YOU ARE THEN, BUT IT SEEMS RATHER A LOT."

"DAT'S JEST GRAND SAH. YO' DE VERY FURST MAN TO COME UP TO DE AVERAGE."

(1935)

First Bright Young Thing (at christening party): "MY HAT! SUPPOSE PHOEBE GIVES ME THE BABY TO NURSE; I'M SURE I SHAN'T KNOW HOW TO HOLD IT."

Second Ditto: "DON'T BE AN ASS; IT'S JUST THE SAME GRIP AS FOR A COCKTAIL-SHAKER."

(1931)

Little Boy (much interested): "OH, MUMMY, DO LET'S WAIT!"

(1927)

AN OLD SONG RESUNG

"OH, I DO LIKE TO BE BESIDE THE SEASIDE—

I DO LIKE TO BE BESIDE THE SEA—

I DO LIKE TO STROLL ALONG THE PROM, PROM, PROM—

WHILE THE BRASS BAND PLAYS TIDDLEY-OM-POM-POM—

SO JUST PUT ME DOWN BESIDE THE SEASIDE—

AND I'LL BE BESIDE MYSELF WITH GLEE—

THERE ARE LOTS OF GIRLS BESIDE I WOULD LIKE TO BE BESIDE—

BESIDE THE SEASIDE, BESIDE THE SEA."

(1938)

Babu Teacher. "NUMBER ONE IS CALLED A 'RIGHT ANGLE,'' AND YOU WOULD NATURALLY SUPPOSE THAT NUMBER TWO IS A 'LEFT ANGLE.' BUT BY ORDER OF GOVERNMENT OF INDIA SURVEY DEPARTMENT THIS IS ALSO A RIGHT ANGLE."

(1924)

The Bosun's Mate (*to new crew*). "NOW I'M GOIN' TO READ OUT SOME O' THE THINGS THE BOARD O' TRADE THINK YOU OUGHT TO KNOW, AN' IF THERE'S ANY OF YOU DON'T UNDERSTAND ENGLISH LET 'IM FIND OUT FROM THE BLOKE NEXT TO 'IM WOT IT'S ALL ABOUT." (1932)

"*Not worth tuppence, Sir? You ought to be here when the tide is in.*" (1935)

STILL LIFE.

ARRANGED BY MR. G. K. CHESTERTON

(1934)

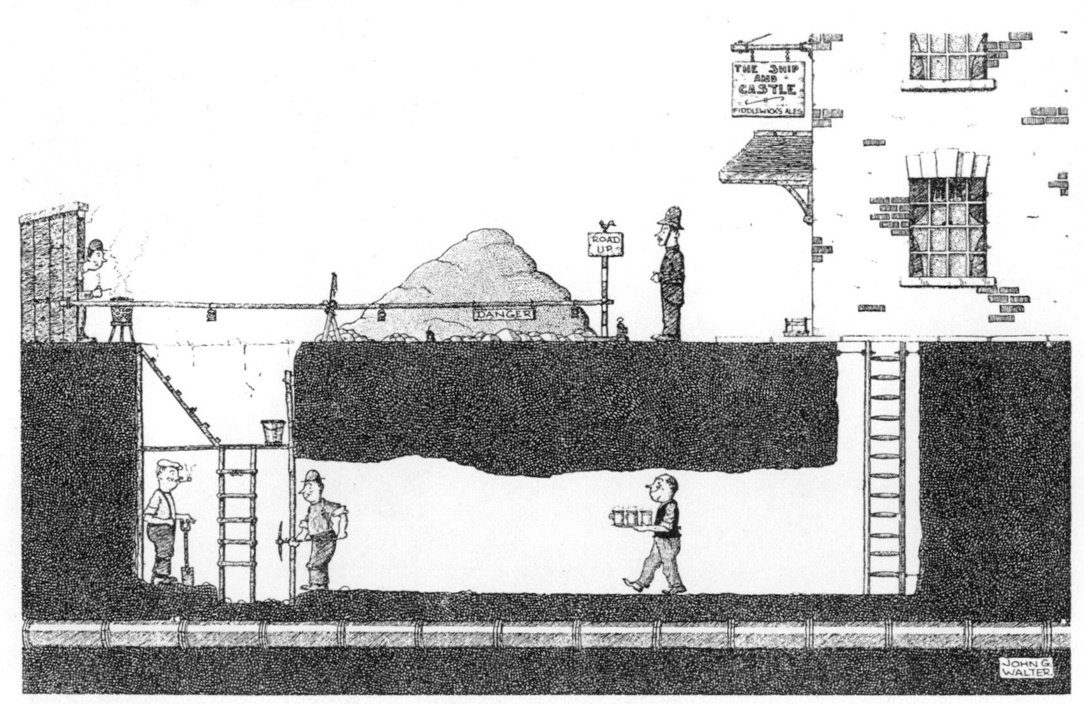

A POSSIBLE SOLUTION OF THE PERENNIAL HOLE-IN-THE-ROAD MYSTERY (1936)

Cyril (referring to total stranger). "I SAY, MABEL, I HOPE THIS CHAP'S ALL RIGHT. ONLY ASLEEP, I MEAN."

Mabel. "WHAT MAKES YOU THINK HE'S ANYTHING ELSE?"

Cyril. "WELL, THIS IS LAST WEDNESDAY'S PAPER."

(1931)

"I must ring off now, darling. I think someone else wants to use the phone." (1939)

"WHERE YOU BEEN?"
" 'AVIN' ME 'AIR CUT."
"YOU KNOW YOU CAN'T 'AVE YER 'AIR CUT IN COMPANY'S TIME."
"WELL, IT GREW IN COMPANY'S TIME, DIDN'T IT?"
"NOT ALL OF IT."
"WELL, I AIN'T HAD IT ALL CUT OFF." (1937)

"Well, which is it, Sam—a lovely old vase or a hideous modern one?"

(1936)

"GOOD LOR', MAN, TAKE YOUR HAT OFF."
"WHY?"
"WELL, ACCORDING TO MY RECKONING WE'RE INSIDE WESTMINSTER ABBEY."

(1937)

"IT TOOK ME NEARLY TEN YEARS TO LEARN THAT I COULDN'T WRITE."
"I SUPPOSE YOU GAVE IT UP THEN?"
"OH, NO! BY THAT TIME I HAD A REPUTATION ESTABLISHED."

(1924)

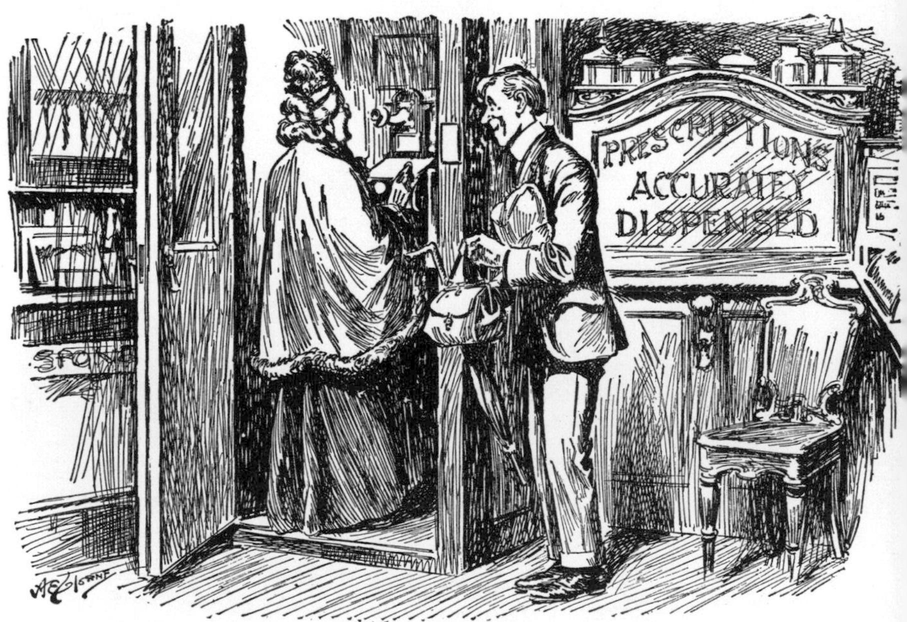

Dear Old Lady (using call-office telephone for the first time, to operator at the Exchange): "AND AS YOU'VE BEEN SO NICE AND ATTENTIVE, MY DEAR, I'M PUTTING AN EXTRA PENNY IN THE BOX FOR YOURSELF."

(1913)

"BUFFALOES, BREAK STEP!"

(1935)

"I've laid out your things to warm by the fire."
(1952)

"My husband's no good as an electrician, but he's terribly clever at carpentry." (1946)

"There's a car like ours." (1954)

I SAY MUMS, WE SHALL BE WANTING SUPPER
WE'LL SAVE SOMETHING FOR YOU DEARS
I SAY MUMMY HAVE WE ANY NaCl ?
IN THE STORE-CUPBOARD DEAR AND DON'T MAKE TOO MUCH MESS
I SAY MOTHER WHERE HAVE THEY PUT MY SPECTACLES ?
HAVE YOU LOOKED IN THE LIBRARY, DEAR
PLEASE MUM, THE WATER WON'T 'OT
HAVE YOU TRIED PUTTING MORE COAL ON?
THE CAT'S BEEN IN THE GREENHOUSE AGAIN, MA'AM
I'M AFRAID YOU WILL HAVE TO THROW IT AWAY
I SAY MATER, IS THERE ANYTHING TO EAT?
THEY'RE KEEPING SOMETHING HOT FOR YOU, DEAR
I SAY MUMMY, WHAT'S A PULMONATE MOLLUSC IN 4 LETTERS?
COULD IT BE 'SLUG', DEAR?
I SAY MA, THESE TROUSERS HAVE NO BUTTONS
COULDN'T YOU CHANGE, DEAR?
I SAY, MUMMY WHAT'S THE FRENCH FOR "HOME"?
'CHEZ' I THINK, DEAR, BUT YOU'D BETTER LOOK IT UP
TD
Thomas Derrick

MOTHER

(1937)

Lady (to Messrs. Cook's official): "I HAVE NOTHING TO DECLARE. WHAT SHALL I SAY?"
Official: "SAY, MADAM, THAT YOU HAVE NOTHING TO DECLARE."
Lady: "YES; BUT SUPPOSE THEY FIND SOMETHING?"
(1913)

Little Daughter (thrilled by Customs-officer's search): "OO-O! HE'S GETTING WARM, ISN'T HE, MUMMY?"
(1933)

"Once you've made the chalk mark, does that mean I've won?"
(1950)

"*It's time we were heading north: Peter Scott's begun to moult.*"

(1956)

(1949)

(1950)

"Please don't get up."
(1952)

(1953)

(1951)

(1948)

THE BRITISH CHARACTER

IMPORTANCE OF TEA

(1935)

(1952)

"I still say if I arrived after lunch I'm entitled to lunch today."

(1955)

(1952)

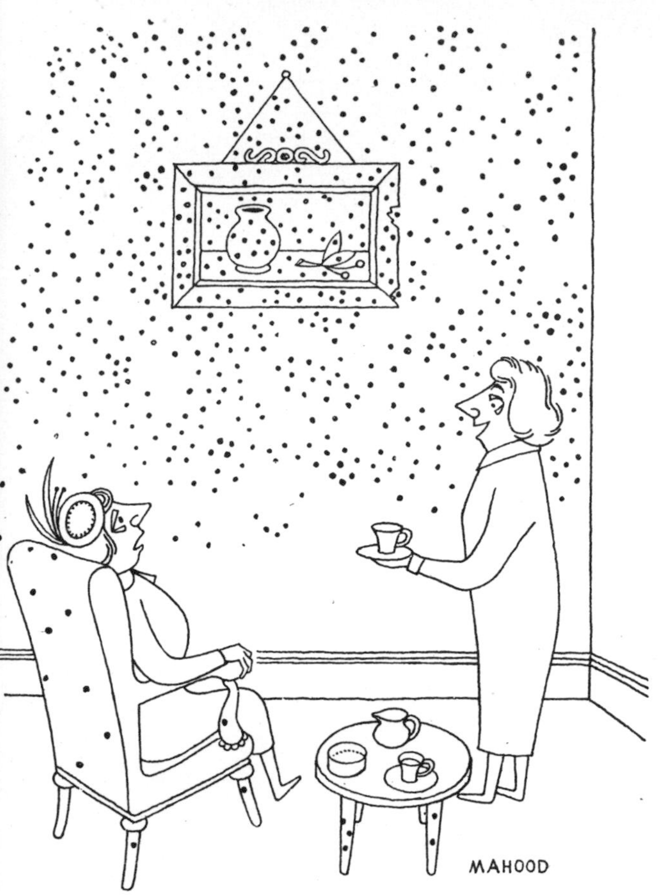

"Oh, no, it's never dull here. There's the cinema and the theatre and, of course, the shooting-gallery next door."

(1950)

"I'm so glad you won. I couldn't have borne another scene like last time."

(1951)

POLICE
WANTED

POLICE
WANTED

POLICE
WANTED

POLICE

"Me? I'm all for playing the National Anthem—gets the place clear in half the time." (1955)

"Oh, good—the News! . . ."

"I'm so sorry, young man. I'd no idea we'd strayed into a military zone."
(1940)

(1940)

(1953)

"Seen my collar, Mildred?"
(1951)

(1954)

(1951)

ffolkes

(1954)

"*That's funny—they* did *say Wednesday, didn't they?*"
(1950)

"*What awkward clown put this switch upside-down?*"
(1942)

(1950)

(1949)

(1947)

"Just run over the whole case-history again —from where you made the mocking remark about the witch doctor." (1946)

"Arbuthnot spent a couple of months in India and doesn't let you forget it for one minute." (1946)

(1955)

"*So much for the bulk of the estate; now for the residue.*"
(1954)

(1949)

"*I find these electric razors save a lot of trouble.*"
(1953)

(1949)

"No, dear, that's not funny."
(1921)

If you have opened the book at this end the drawing above is not for you. You have 351 pages to go before agreeing or disagreeing with the caption.